TRUTH
THAT MATTERS

*The
Bible's Message
for You*

KEAVIN HAYDEN

Pacific Press Publishing Association
Nampa, Idaho
Oshawa, Ontario, Canada

Edited by Kenneth R. Wade
Designed by Tim Larson
Cover photo by Marc Muench/Tony Stone Images

Copyright © 1997 by
Pacific Press Publishing Association
Printed in the United States of America
All Rights Reserved

Accuracy of all quotations and references is the responsibility of the author.

ISBN 0-8163-1393-8

97 98 99 00 01 • 5 4 3 2 1

DEDICATION

To my precious wife and best friend, Lisa,
an honest seeker of truth,
for your unwavering example
of conscientiousness in following
what you knew to be right.
I will always love and forever be indebted to you.
Thank you for the years of happiness
you've brought to my life.

CONTENTS

FOREWORD

When, in departing, Bill Haley said to the audience, "God bless you!" I was taken aback. I had just joined the Comets, and we were performing in the Forum, a nightclub in Jacksonville, Florida. The statement seemed so out of place. The atmosphere seemed less than holy, not to mention the performers, including myself.

Bill did the same thing at the conclusion of every show. This did not appear to offend anyone, that is, if they were capable of hearing anything by the time the reveling ended. But it didn't make any sense. It appeared that it was just an "off-the-cuff" saying thrown out to make the revelers content. At least it seemed that way to me, for no one knew better than I the lifestyles we were all living—lifestyles that completely militated against anything that savored of religion.

This conundrum was not new to me. In fact, I grew up with this double vision. There was the priest from the local parish who came around to court the boys on my block. Then there was Wally, the altar boy who swore worse than a sailor. On the other side of the street there was Maury, who took me to his synagogue, where he proceeded to steal the rabbi's wine out of the refrigerator. Not able to reconcile these disparities, I found myself imbibing an array of philosophies and theories that ultimately made me cynical and caused me to question the genuineness of religion. However, there was something in my innermost soul that craved for that which rang true—something that could turn all the plasticity of life into genuine reality. But where could this be found? Certainly, I thought, not in religion.

Many have felt the same longing, but they, too, have been turned off by the pretentious and oftentimes hypocritical menu offered by those who are religious. Thousands have turned away from religion and have gone to different cisterns hoping to satisfy this innate craving. However, these cisterns soon run dry, leaving the soul withered and barren. Many people just give up and declare their quest for truth vain and pointless. Still, they may hear a haunting whisper in their minds, declaring that maybe there is something missing.

Keavin Hayden spent his early life struggling with the same frustrations and disappointments I encountered in my search. Believing, however, that there must be a way to reach the goal, he persisted until he arrived at his most profound discovery. Finally he concluded that religion is its own greatest antagonist.

Keavin's sharing in *Truth That Matters* is provocative. He is both poignant and straightforward. He does not attack anyone or any system of belief. Rather, he seeks to remove the debris that has obstructed our path to truth. His simple, down-to-earth approach at leading the reader to the ultimate conclusion is refreshing.

Louis R. Torres
Former Bass Player with Bill Haley and the Comets

ACKNOWLEDGMENTS

Too numerous to mention are the people who had a part in the mission of this book. But I do wish especially to acknowledge the contributions of several people. David Merrill and Dr. Jack Blanco, for reading and critiquing the manuscript. Dr. Blanco is the author of *The Clear Word*. Because I feel this paraphrase makes the Bible easy to understand, I have quoted from it frequently. Unless otherwise noted, texts are taken from *The Clear Word*.

To Ed and Arlene Jensen, for your unfailing inspiration, willing attitude, and professional work when it was needed the most.

And last, a special thanks to Ken Wade and my friends at Pacific Press Publishing Association, for your vision and dedicated service in getting this book out to the masses.

To all those who participated in this project, I want to say, "Thank you." A part of your life is certainly interwoven throughout these pages.

Keavin Hayden

CHAPTER ONE

Is the Devil for Real?

My mother's voice sounded a little shaky as I answered the phone. "Keavin, something really strange happened to me the other day. The few people I've told say I'm crazy, but I wanted to tell you." She knew that I had recently begun studying about the spiritual world.

"The other day I was canning beans at home by myself," she continued, "and went up to the attic to get some jars. As I climbed down the stairs, I turned and saw someone standing at the end of the hallway. Startled, I said 'Oh, you scared me!' Then the figure suddenly disappeared. The whole thing made me feel so uneasy that I left the house to find your father. Even he was a little skeptical of the story, but, Keavin, I know what I saw!"

She said that for several years she had been hearing strange noises in the attic. Fear often prickled her skin with goose bumps when she climbed the stairs. However, this experience changed her superstition into an understandable concern.

I must say something here in defense of my

mother. Anyone who knows her would bear witness that she fully possesses her sanity. I had absolutely no doubts as to the validity of her experience. I had no explanation, but as I hung up the phone, I continued to think about what she had said.

Over the next few weeks I shared the story with several people whom I knew had studied deeply into the Bible and its teachings. They told me of a spiritual warfare going on in our world between the powers of good and evil. One friend asked if there might be any old rock-and-roll records or tapes in the house. If so, that would give evil spirits the right to be on the premises. I then remembered that when I moved from my parents' home seven years earlier I had left behind several albums and posters dealing with the rock culture.

I will admit that as my friend explained this spiritual battle, I had my doubts. It all sounded too strange. Surely there was a more logical explanation. But I had decided to investigate all possible leads, so I called my mother. "Mom," I asked, "What did you do with all that stuff I left in my room when I moved out for college?" Her reply gave me chills—"Oh, I put it all up in the attic!" I then explained to her all that I had learned and told her I would be home soon to clean out the attic. She eagerly gave her consent.

Some weeks later my wife and I arrived at my parents' house. Because one end of the long attic was without light, I grabbed a flashlight and quickly climbed the stairs, my wife hanging tightly onto my arm. We came to an area where I turned on a light and found the boxes I had packed several years before. Sure enough, inside were the tapes, albums, and picture posters of my teenage idols. We put them all in a garbage bag and then headed for the darker part of the attic loft.

Stepping slowly along, we both began to feel a tingling sensation come over our bodies. I shined the flashlight along the wall and spotted a tall stack of family board games we had played when we were growing up. Then my feet stumbled on something in the darkness. As I shined the light down, we saw—to our chilling surprise—the mysterious, veil-faced woman of the "Ouija" board.

Suddenly I thought of the Christmas long ago when my brother had received the game and how we used to sit around it asking our silly questions. But the question I had now didn't seem so silly. "Were there really unseen evil spirits around us as we stood there in that attic staring at this tool of the occult world?"

One thing was certain: I was not going to consult the "Ouija" to get my answer! So I asked my wife, and we agreed on the solution: Get that thing out of the attic!

After returning downstairs I asked my mother, "What do you know about the "Ouija" board?" Her reply leads us to our discussion in this chapter. She said, "I've heard it's of the devil."

Is the devil for real, or is he just a figment of man's fascination? An old adage says, "If there really was a devil, he would be the last to tell you." How, then, can anyone know for sure that such a creature even exists? According to the Bible, there is indeed a real, literal being called the devil. And since that Book contains the original source of information documenting his existence, its teachings need to be considered.

How the war began

The very first verse of the Bible tells us, "In the beginning God created the heavens and the earth" (Genesis 1:1, NIV). And the New Testament Scriptures tell us exactly who this creative God is. Speaking of Jesus Christ, the apostle Paul wrote, "For by him all things were created that are in heaven and that are on earth, visible and invisible" (Colossians 1:16, NIV).

The Bible tells us of events that took place in heaven before God created our earth. There God had established a society of angels and a government designed to best meet their needs. The uniqueness of this governmental structure was that it operated on the principle of each created being having in mind not his own interests but rather the interests of others. No angel needed to be selfishly absorbed in taking care of himself, for his needs were the priority of everyone around him. And in a special sense, Christ had the ability and capacity to meet the needs, both great and small, of each of His created beings. Everything essential to their welfare was provided. Nothing that could add to their happiness was withheld. Like a caring father who loves his children and whose highest desire in life is to please them, so God ruled over His marvelous kingdom. Perfect freedom, perfect security, perfect contentment, was the possession of all who lived in this heavenly paradise.

Within the government there were positions of responsibility and authority that Christ had assigned. One angel in particular had been placed in a most special position—that of ministering in the very throne room of God! This angel's name was Lucifer, and God had endowed him with special abilities, enabling him to reveal to others the ever-unfolding attributes of God's beautiful character. Perhaps that is why the Bible, in describing Lucifer, says that he was "full of wisdom and perfect in beauty" (Ezekiel 28:12, NIV). Though Lucifer's position, abilities, and beauty exceeded that of the ordinary angels, these facts did not bother them, because they realized that through Lucifer's special attributes, they could gain new and special insights concerning their Creator.

You see, Christ the Creator was a very special

person in the eyes of the angelic throngs because of who He was. He was the Master Creator—the Maker who ruled not only over them but over all creation. Only He had the power and ability to hang the multitudes of worlds in space and assign these heavenly bodies their orbits. He alone had given the angels their own existence. Also, Christ possessed wonderful charms that no other being could possibly possess. And it was His charming personality that won the respect, reverence, and willing allegiance of the angels. None ever questioned His motives and purposes, for all knew Him to be unselfish, courteous, and fair. This marvelous being called Christ was so adored and admired by the angels that each waited with anxious heart to do something special for Him. Carrying out His requests was the highest satisfaction to which they could attain. To be in His presence was the loftiest joy to which they could aspire. And it was this bonded relationship between each of the angels and the Creator that made heaven the happy place it was.

But trouble invaded this paradise of love when Lucifer's attitude mysteriously began to change. He started entertaining thoughts and suppositions that were not in harmony with his holy nature. He suddenly became keenly aware of the special attention the heavenly host were giving to Christ. And now like the common schoolboy who becomes maddened over the fact that a classmate is naturally endowed with enamoring charms and abilities, Lucifer began to feel envious and jealous of Christ. The result of this envy in Lucifer's heart was a spirit of distrust toward his Creator. He thought that perhaps God was only using him in order to gain more adoration for Himself from the angels.

The Bible teaches us that Lucifer finally arrived at the place where his main obsession was to be viewed by others as equal with God. He wanted to be the object of their grandest adoration and most reverent worship. In revealing these inner thoughts of Lucifer, the Scriptures say, "How you are fallen from heaven, O Lucifer, son of the morning. . . . For you have said in your heart: 'I will ascend into heaven, I will exalt my throne above the stars of God . . . I will be like the Most High'" (Isaiah 14:12-14, NKJV). Thus the creature sought to prove himself as important and honorable as the Creator.

But realistically, Lucifer's desire to become God was an impossibility. The Scriptures clearly teach that Christ Himself had no beginning. In other words, He was not created. Rather, He *was* the Creator, the very One who brought all creatures, including Lucifer, into existence. And, the creature can never be the Creator. The two are as different in relationship as the moon is from the sun. Though the moon has the ability to reflect whatever light it receives from the sun, even at its brightest it can never be the sun. Just so, God's creatures can reflect different aspects of God's character in various degrees, but they can never be God. Yet Lucifer for so long visualized himself as being in the place of God that to him the literal distinction between the creature and the Creator became blurred. The more he thought about becoming God, the less impossible it seemed.

Lucifer eventually finalized his decision to reject the authority of his Creator and rebel against Him by trying to overthrow Christ's position. He would use his esteemed position among the angels in an effort to turn them against God. But he knew the angels highly reverenced Christ. Therefore, he must begin his ambitious campaign with covert methods. So he began portraying himself as being highly interested in helping God make heaven a better society in which to live. But while acting as an advocate for improving the welfare state of the angels, he artfully planted in their minds the seeds of his own distrust toward God. He insinuated that under the present order of things, they would never really come to understand what true freedom was all about. Thus he sought to lead them to believe that their present state of existence was one of bondage.

For the longest time, this self-seeking angel went about subtly laboring to fulfill his strong, secret desire for advancement. And when he felt that the seeds of distrust had been well placed in the hearts of heaven's inhabitants, Lucifer launched into open rebellion. He boldly began a slander campaign against Christ. His propaganda openly charged Christ with possessing all the self-serving attributes the rebel angel himself now actually possessed. He painted God as One who was only out for Himself and directly challenged His ability and right to rule over creation. With lies that stemmed from intense hatred and jealousy, the once-happy angel maligned and brought grief to the heart of God, who had forever maintained only feelings of generous affection for His creatures.

Thus the selfless society of heaven—the place where everyone sought only to meet the needs of others—was invaded by a spirit of selfishness. A new element called evil had now, for the first time, entered the universe. And the great angel known as Lucifer received a new name, "Satan," which means "an evil accuser or slanderer." As a result, it is recorded that war broke out in heaven. The defective angel won one-third of the stars (heavenly angels) to his side with his anti-Christ propaganda (see Revelation 12:3, 4. Dragon = Satan [See Revelation 12:9] and stars = angels). The book of Revelation gives an account of what happened next.

"This controversy between God and the dragon began years ago in heaven. God's Son Michael [an angelic name for Christ] and the loyal angels fought against the dragon and his angels. The dragon and his angels were not strong enough, so they lost their place in heaven. *The great dragon that was defeated and cast out of heaven with his angels was Satan,* that ancient serpent also called the devil. He and his angels were hurled to the earth and are trying to deceive the whole world" (Revelation 12:7-9, emphasis supplied).

So the Scriptures teach that God did not create a devil but a beautiful, perfect angel named Lucifer. And this story of Lucifer's defection is the biblical explanation of how sin began. Sin was not created by God; rather, it evolved in Lucifer's heart by the process of his own choices. Then it spread, infecting myriads of angels and eventually the inhabitants of our own planet.

At this point many ask, "Why didn't God go ahead and destroy the devil and his angels and blot out evil from existence? Why did He allow sin to spread?" Although the answers to such questions are too complex for the human mind to fully comprehend, we must understand that Satan had cloaked his evil intentions under an appearance of trying to do good. Even though his Creator knew what his true motives were, many angels as well as inhabitants of other worlds were watching, and they couldn't clearly discern who was right and who was wrong. Because of this, it was necessary for God to let the process of evil come to full maturity. And it was our planet that received that evil seed as it fell from heaven. It is here where sin's final results are now being witnessed. No one can deny that we live in a world full of evil and much sorrow.

War comes to earth

The Bible not only offers an explanation as to how sin began in heaven; it also depicts how it was transferred to our planet.

Most people are familiar with the story of Adam and Eve and the Garden of Eden (see Genesis, chapters 2 and 3). Though many regard the story as allegorical, the Bible presents it as authentic. It offers the only reasonable explanation as to why we see so much evil, sickness, and sorrow around us today. Though we will not go into detail concerning Eden's story, we do need to understand the issues behind what happened there.

God dearly loved Adam and Eve. He came to visit them every day, in order to spend special time with them in meeting their needs. As He had done for the angels in heaven, Christ had provided everything necessary for their happiness.

Now the story of the Fall tells us that Satan disguised himself as a beautiful, talking serpent and led Eve into sin. Then through her, Adam was led to disobey and turn away from the God he loved. But God had given them clear warnings concerning Satan and his work of evil. If they had only followed God's advice, it would have protected them from the devil's temptations. But they willfully ventured on forbidden ground to the "tree of the knowledge of good and evil" (see Genesis 2:16, 17; 3:1-13).

Here Satan led them to think that God was withholding essential information from them. That information was called the "knowledge . . . of evil." But Christ knew that such knowledge would only destroy them, just as it had destroyed His beloved angels who had already fallen. So, out of love and concern He had warned Eden's occupants that the inherent result of eating the forbidden fruit would be subjection to death. But they chose to believe Satan instead, when he told them, "Ye shall not surely die" (Genesis

3:4, KJV). They violated the great law of love by self-ishly trying to gain something for themselves—by attempting to become gods (see Genesis 3:5). By their disobedience they obtained a practical knowledge of sin and opened the door for death and evil to flood our world. By their fatal decision, the entire human race was sold into bondage and by nature became the servants of sin and its originator, the devil himself.

But God in mercy provided an opportunity for Adam and his offspring to escape this bondage. He opened a way so all humans would have the ability to choose for themselves which army they would serve in—God's or Satan's. Yes, all of us decide our own future, depending upon how we choose to relate to the spiritual battle between the forces of good and evil in our world. No wonder religion is such an explosive topic! By how we choose to live our lives, we determine who our spiritual leader is.

Even here the devil has the advantage, for to be on God's team one must make a definite choice. All of us choose either directly or indirectly. There is absolutely no middle or neutral ground. In fact, the Bible teaches that we are born in Satan's camp and the only way we will ever leave it is to choose to do so. But when we do make a decision against him, God can then begin to work in our behalf in the spiritual realms. He has the power to limit Satan's workings in our lives. Just as when we took the Ouija board out of my mother's attic, she ceased to be troubled by the demonic activities that had been going on. One can see, then, why the master of deception is thrilled when he can convince people that neither he nor God exists—for then they never realize the necessity of leaving his ranks.

Despite the fact that some preachers still continue

to warn about the devil from their pulpits, our culture is becoming increasingly fascinated, focused, and fixated on Satan. Songwriters write about him, Hollywood fantasizes of him, and each October, parents even dress up their children in costumes they think resemble him. Interest in the occult—and even full-blown Satan worship—is now on the increase worldwide.

However, most people would never consciously assent to worship and serve the devil. Therefore, Satan knows he must gain their homage in the same way he persuaded the angels in heaven—by deception and trickery. His plan of attack is simple—lie about God and lie about himself.

First, he tries to blame much of evil's destructiveness on God. When bad things happen, God usually gets the blame. When bad weather or fires destroy life and property, the insurance companies call it an "act of God." Satan also portrays God as cruel and unforgiving. He wants people to think God gets great satisfaction out of seeing the human race suffer—to see Him as one just waiting to get even with us. Therefore, many believe that God is only out for Himself and has no real interest in the lives of men. By these means, men are led to view God as their enemy. Thus, through the centuries, the devil has been very successful in turning multitudes away from God.

Another very profitable campaign for him has been to cover up his own identity by creating a false image of himself. I remember back in my hometown a high school whose sports teams were known as the Owensboro Red Devils. Their mascot was a shady-looking creature dressed in red and black, complete with horns, goatee, and arrow-shaped tail. Sporting an evil grin on his face, he carried his favorite weapon—the notorious pitchfork. Everybody feared competition with the Red Devils. Yet little did any of us know in those days of high school activities that even the slightest contemplation of such an image was weakening our ability to detect the devil's true appearance. Without a doubt, the devil is most devilish when he is disguised and undetected. Even William Shakespeare acknowledged:

> "The spirit that I have seen
> may be the devil; and the devil hath
> power to assume a pleasing shape"
> (*Hamlet*, Act ii, scene 2).

Satan's strategy is quite simple. If those who believe the devil exists can be programmed to be on their guard for an ugly, terrifying creature, they will more easily open their door to his impostors claiming to be sent from God. Paul, the great Christian apostle, wrote, "Satan was once an angel of light and he can still appear to look like one. So it's no great thing for those who have allowed themselves to be influenced by the evil one to make themselves look like men of righteousness" (2 Corinthians 11:14, 15).

Yes, it is a fact that the most covert way the devil will approach you is through professed Christians with their Bibles in hand. Jesus gave the warning this way: "Be on your guard against false religious teachers, who come to you dressed up as sheep but are really greedy wolves" (Matthew 7:15, Phillips).

The truth of our discussion is this: Whether we acknowledge it or not, there really is a devil. Certainly no one has ever proved that he does not exist. Even though our sensory powers are too weak to see him, he is there. To believe otherwise would allow him to do whatever he wanted in our lives. Like a thief robbing the house of a blind and deaf man, all he then has to do to accomplish our destruction is to avoid bumping into us. But though we cannot see the devil, the great God of love has given us the Bible, which unveils Satan and his plan of attacking us. Like a watchdog that calls attention to the thief's approach, the Bible reveals Satan's strategy.

Yet there is a reason some prefer to believe he doesn't exist. Such a belief aids in blurring the vision of good and evil, right and wrong, a holy God and a sinful devil. It helps excuse any hints of evil we might detect within ourselves. Then with no barometer of right or wrong, the conclusion is that since there is no devil, there probably is no God to whom we must answer either. Therefore we can safely do as we feel, for in the end we will only have to give answer to ourselves. To acknowledge the devil would be to challenge this self-gratifying belief of no accountability, for if the devil exists, then so does God.

However, the most convincing way to prove Satan's existence is to make a firm decision to leave his army and take a stand under the banner of his most hated enemy—Jesus Christ. Then the reality of this whole story will be experienced firsthand. Only then can one fully identify with what the apostle Peter meant when he said, "Stay alert and keep your eyes open because the devil is roaming around like a hungry lion, desperate to find anyone he can destroy" (1 Peter 5:8).

CHAPTER TWO

The Man From Outer Space

"I think we should invite him home for lunch. Remember, the Bible says we should not forget to entertain strangers, for in so doing some have entertained angels and didn't know it."

"Yes, Mommy, this man might be an angel!"

My wife carefully listened to my young daughter and me as the church services were letting out. We had been discussing whether or not we should invite a stranger who had shown up at church home with us for lunch.

"OK," agreed my wife, "let's go ask him."

The man eagerly accepted the invitation, and within the hour we were sitting in our kitchen. While my wife worked on the final preparations for our meal, I sat and talked with our guest.

Being intrigued with people's backgrounds, I asked him, "So, where do you come from?" I was totally unprepared for his answer.

"My place of origin is not on your planet."

"Excuse me?" I said, trying not to show any strange facial expressions.

"That's right," he continued, "though you may find

it hard to believe, I come from a planet in a galaxy far away from this one. This is actually my second visit to earth. Last year I landed in East Germany, and since that time have been traveling extensively throughout Planet Earth."

With that, my wife, who had been listening in on our conversation, dropped the salad bowl. As she looked at me I was tempted to think that maybe she was from another planet, because her facial color was now nearly green with discomfort. (I don't know what color I was radiating!)

Then I looked back at our guest, hoping to see him break out in laughter and tell us he was only joking. But the dead stare in his eyes and the straightness of his face told me he was serious.

I have often since thought about that experience and am continually amazed at the power science fiction has had upon the minds of this generation. We have been programmed to consider the impossible, while at the same time we've been taught to be skeptical of anything we cannot see.

And though I knew our visitor that day was but following the ideas of his own imagination, the Bible says there was a man who once visited our planet— and He did not originate from our world. They called Him Jesus Christ, and the only way one can truly accept the validity of His story is by means of a faith that is based upon reason.

Romans 10:17 says that "faith comes from listening to what God has to say, including what he told us about the Lord Jesus Christ in His word." So the words found in the Bible are as seeds of faith that germinate, take root, and eventually bring forth the fruit of a changed life. To the possessor of such faith, the story of Jesus Christ becomes vividly real. Faith changes his or her attitude, habits, words, and actions—even lifelong plans. Thus the Christian often becomes the object of ridicule by family and friends because his or her behavior is guided by principles that others cannot see or understand. But to such a follower, God reveals Himself through the imagination and life experiences, which leads to faith that keeps growing stronger.

Satan knows that this simple faith in God will lead souls out of his captivity. He is the god of this world, and to mankind he is a most dangerous foe. When Adam forfeited his right to dominion over this earth, he passed it into the hands of Satan, who began using the planet as a military base to carry on his cosmic warfare against heaven. Also, by choosing to sin, Adam pulled the plug from God, the only Source of life, and subjected future generations to death and the tyranny of the devil. Though originally created in the pure and holy image of God, Adam could now only pass on to his children his new image, which included a rebellious attitude toward God. Now, like the Europeans under Nazi control in the 1940s, the human race was helpless to break out of Satan's grip. Man's only hope was that an outside force would invade captive Earth and liberate it from the devil.

God sends help

After recounting man's fall, the rest of the Bible's pages are devoted to the story of a God who loved His lost Creation more than He loved Himself. It unfolds His plan to save man from the devil's control and restore the earth to its sinless, happy state. That plan is called Salvation.

But God's military strategy of invading earth was unlike any the world has ever known. It did not call for fleets of ships, columns of tanks, horizons filled with aircraft, or huge armies of foot soldiers. No, it consisted of a vulnerable, helpless Baby in a mother's arms.

Still, in the minds of men and women today a stigma seems to exist when it comes to understanding God's attitude toward us. We so often think of God as One who keeps Himself aloof from our troubled lives; as someone who takes pleasure in seeing us agonize, thinking that we are getting just what we deserve. Since we cannot see God, Satan lies to us about what He is like. He portrays God as being cruel and unjust, because the Bible says that someday He will have no other option but to destroy all sinners who will not live in obedience to Him. Thus, many are compelled to serve God out of fear rather than love and respect. However, God is not out to destroy us but to destroy sin.

The Bible clearly describes God's attitude and yearning desire toward sinful humans. It says that "He loves everyone, even the wicked, and He doesn't want anyone to lose out on heaven but to turn from their sins and be saved" (2 Peter 3:9b).

If our lives are condemned in the end, it won't be because God condemns us but because we condemn ourselves. Scripture makes very clear that "God didn't send His Son to the world to condemn people, but to forgive them and to save them. Those who believe in Him will no longer need to live under condemnation. But those who do not believe in the Son of God can't be healed because they don't believe. What condemns people is not the fact that they're in darkness, but that they don't accept the light of truth. People don't want to be told that their nature is evil so they don't come to the light, because they're more comfortable with darkness than with light. But those who are honest with themselves will come to the Son of Man for help. They want to be changed and are willing for him to change them" (John 3:17-21).

Oh, how different our lives would be if we but fully understood what God is really like! His truest feelings toward us are sincere, tender, full of sympathy and pity. His most intense desire is to help us. Whether we realize it or not, our Creator identifies with our bitterest experiences just as though He Himself were the one going through them. To Jesus, heaven was not a place to be desired while we were lost. Think about it. God couldn't get us off His mind. The misery of our hopeless plight reached into the depths of His very own heart. So, for our sakes, He left the security and pleasures of heaven and came to our sin-stained planet to make a way to bring us back home. God Himself actually entered into the experience of sorrowful humanity—the Creator became the creature and placed Himself in enemy territory in order to win back His fallen race from the devil.

Pictures of God

Even as a man, Christ defeated the devil by not yielding to His many temptations to sin. By a life of faithful obedience, Christ revealed God's true character. In every village Jesus entered, He demonstrated God's love toward the fallen race. He pitied the most degraded and despised of society's outcasts. He restored sight to the blind, caused the lame to walk, opened the ears of the deaf, freed up the tongues of the speechless, and raised people's loved ones from the dead. He even took time to notice and bless the little children. But most important, He unlocked the chains of guilt that were crushing out the spirit of men's souls. This He did by assuring people that He, by the power He possessed as God, would forgive their sins if by faith they believed in Him. Thus the Saviour's whole life on earth was lived to bless others by showing them how much God really cared for them. Like a walking video screen, He was constantly flashing picture images of the true character of the unseen God before fallen humanity.

Naturally, His life aroused the devil's opposition. The barriers of deception he had erected between the people and God were quickly being broken down. Throngs of people began flocking to Jesus. Both day and night found Him ministering to the hurts and needs of sinners and winning them back to God. If Jesus were to continue living, it surely wouldn't be long before the whole world would recognize Satan's misrepresentations about God. Satan worked against Jesus by inspiring men whose own earthly positions were challenged by Jesus to hate Him and finally to crucify Him.

Yet even in death, Jesus was victorious. Because He was willing to die for sins He did not commit, He could now exchange His record of a pure, sinless life for Adam's and our sinful records. Because of His willingness to assume the death of guilty men, sinners themselves could choose the punishment He bore as full payment on their sinful debt and justly receive God's offer of eternal life. The writer of the book of Hebrews made this transactional point clear when he wrote, "So even though he was God's own Son, His obedience had to be tested by daily suffering and eventual death, and having passed the obedience test, He became a complete sacrifice for our sins and the source of eternal salvation to all those who trust God and obey Him" (Hebrews 5:8, 9).

God now offers us this incredible opportunity of eternal life as a free gift by means of a faith that wholeheartedly believes the whole thing is true. We must learn to live as those who "do not look at the things which are seen, but at the things which are not seen. For the things which are seen are temporary, but the things which are not seen are eternal" (2 Corinthians 4:18, NKJV). This offer of salvation cannot be seen. It cannot be earned by appeasing God through anything we do; neither can it be bought with any amount of money. If it could, there is no question that more people would obtain it. But then salvation's plan would become corrupted by extortion, bribery, and fraud. Therefore, God in His wisdom has ordained that we can be forgiven our past sins only through faith in the life, death, and resurrection of His Son Christ Jesus.

Conditions to salvation's contract

Though we cannot do anything to earn this forgiveness, certain conditions must be met in order to activate the principles of saving grace in our lives. Try as the devil may to keep us from God by causing us to doubt His willingness to forgive, if these conditions are met, we may with absolute assurance trust that we are forgiven and are heirs of eternal life. What God requires of us is simple and reasonable: confession of our sinful ways, a willingness to give them up (repentance), and belief in God's promise to forgive.

But there is a major roadblock to publicly coming to Christ and confessing our sinfulness and need for Him. That obstacle is the self-imagery we have constructed for ourselves. Self-imagery involves how people decide to relate to society around them. It's a public statement of who we are and what values we hold. It works like this:

A person, through the influences of society around him, decides what image he wants for himself. This choice of image is most strongly motivated by how he wants to be viewed by other people. Then he sets out to live up to that image. The degree of education, the living environment, the circle of friends, the style of dress, the model of car, the mannerisms and thought processes all are determined by the image chosen. Most people invest their entire lives in trying to live out their dream and once established will do whatever it takes to hold onto their self-erected images. Thus this expression of self serves as a growth medium for pride, selfishness, conceit, denial, egotism, bigotry, adultery, envy and jealousy, hatred, greed, dishonesty, depression, and suicide.

With all of us, this self-imagery becomes nothing more than an attempt to cover up our real hurts and sorrows. We have learned well how to hide what we don't want others to know and see. Self-imaging has proven to be one of the most effective means of squelching the cries of the innermost soul. But it is like a drug that temporarily relieves the pain but can't cure the disease.

The truth of Christ's Word, and its revelation of our need for Him, is a direct challenge to our self-projected images. To acknowledge this would mean deflating our self-inflated egos. It is because of this that many refuse to respond to God's offer of eternal salvation. But the gospel call seems to truly appeal to those who long for a change in their lives, to those who are tired of playing in the social sandboxes of this world, to those who are willing to acknowledge and confess their need of a Saviour. Thus it often appears to the worldling that only the weak embrace religion. But the truth is that such have simply not come to grips with their own weakness. Instead, many desperately try to act as if they have it all together, when deep down, they know they do not. Because a public confession of our need often humiliates us by bashing that image of self, few ever truly make a genuine decision for Christ.

Yet even this humiliating condition of accepting Christ has been made easy by the religious social clubs found in churches all over America. A shallow profession of Christ that requires no sacrifice of our selfish lives is often a popular move. But false professors who think themselves good and hang on to their façades will be shocked in the end to find that many of the drunkards, drug addicts, prostitutes, and mentally unstable will inherit heaven while they themselves will be left out. Why? Because those who bottom out in life seem more likely to recognize their need than the self-sufficient. They have no reputations to uphold, and they take full advantage of the Saviour's offer to wipe clean the darkened, depressive slates of their past and give them a fresh, new start.

New people

Once people have come to understand God's forgiving plan and have accepted it, then the devil presents to them still another subtle lie. He tells them they may continue living the same way they did before they knew Christ and God will overlook it because He loves them so much. This is a most popular deception in Christian circles today and a major cause of hypocrisy.

We must understand that one of the conditions of salvation is repentance. That word literally means to come to hate something enough to want to stop doing it. If it is sin in our lives that we are to be repenting of, then why would we think we can safely continue doing what we know is wrong?

If we find ourselves still loving things that we know are wrong, we need not despair. The Bible teaches that it is God who gives repentance to us. The fact that we now see our wrong is evidence that God is working in our lives. We only need to be open and honest with Him and acknowledge the fact that we still love these sins but really want to hate them. Then if we will but continue to pray and contemplate His love for us, we will eventually come to hate the things we once loved and love the things we once hated. God will cause us to become new people with new desires, motives, and purposes. Our highest goal will then be to love and obey God by following His plan for our lives. Our greatest effort will be to live a pure life just as Jesus did.

Though most of our friends and family won't understand the changes taking place in us, we ourselves will know that these changes are the result of seeing the folly of our former lives. As we confess our need and unworthiness, believe in Christ's forgiving love, and seek a new determination to live aright, we take the first steps of faith in a genuine Christian experience. Anything short of this will be as phony as trying to convince people we're from another planet. Maturing, honest-hearted Christians will never be satisfied to play the religious games of hypocritical Christianity. They will not be boasting of their religious piety while their minds are dwelling on the golf course, the afternoon ball games, or the shopping malls even before the church service ends. They have found something better and more fascinating than all the distractions of this earth. They truly understand what it cost God to get them back, and they feel humbled and honored to be counted so valuable.

A beautiful illustration of this new relationship with God is seen in the story of a slave who was taken to auction. He had been there too often and was finally fed up with the degrading process. As the bidding started, he began yelling out, "I ain't a gonna work! I ain't a gonna work!" Of course this cry didn't increase his value in the minds of the bidders, but finally a wealthy plantation owner bought this bondman whom others now counted as worthless.

As the owner loaded his new slave into the wagon and started driving home, the slave spoke to him in very hateful tones saying, "I ain't a gonna work for you, white man." The new owner said nothing. Finally he pulled up in front of a small, well-kept cabin surrounded with beds of beautifully cultivated flowers. Then as the shackles were unlocked and the antiwork sentiments continued, the owner informed the slave that he had bought him to set him free. The cabin was to be his place of peaceful retirement. The tired and often-abused slave could hardly believe his ears. But it was true, he was receiving the freedom of which he had dreamed his whole life. Then, with eyes full of appreciation, he fell weeping at the man's feet and cried out, "Master, I'll serve you forever!"

That is the attitude of those who truly experience Christ's redemptive power of love in their lives. They have been forgiven and set free from their past of serving Satan and their own slavish natures. They realize that God gave His life in service for them, and now they gladly consent to a life of obedience and servitude to Him.

I want to personally appeal to everyone reading this book. Please understand that I know all too well the emptiness that attends life when the party is over and the guests have gone home, when the noise of the television or stereo is needed to drown out the conscience that is trying to speak to us about life's realities. But I also know from experience the peace and joy that comes from finally going all the way with God.

You may be an old friend who didn't understand the changes that took place in my life years ago. You may be someone I don't even know who is now contemplating suicide because no one seems to care. Maybe you are someone who senses your need because of a recent divorce, illness, or the death of someone you loved. Or you may be just sick and tired of living the lie. Whoever you are, wherever you are, and whatever your circumstances, I just want to assure you that God cares and is patiently waiting with the answers to all your life's problems. He's anxiously waiting to forgive you of your past, no matter what you've done or how bad you've been. He wants to give you another opportunity to start over. But He's also asking you to be honest with both Him and yourself. The first step toward Him begins on our knees with a sinner's prayer. I invite you to pray it. Just kneel before God alone and believe that He will hear.

> Lord, I thought I was good, but I'm not,
> I thought I knew best for me, but I didn't,
> I now confess my need for you.
> Please change my heart's motives and desires.
> Please forgive me of my past life of sin,
> of running from you.
> And Lord, I believe you hear me and will answer my prayer.
> In Jesus' name, Amen.

CHAPTER THREE

The Party's Almost Over

The king sat upon his royal throne. Before him were seated a thousand of the most important men in the kingdom. Around him everywhere could be seen the most beautiful and seductive women the country could produce. Every kind of food and strong drink imaginable invited all to the banqueting tables. The palace air resonated with laughter and excitement. The party had begun.

It really doesn't matter that the year was 539 B. C., for the world has always loved a good party. I'm sure the teenage Babylonian king, Belshazzar, could have partied with any of today's rip-roaring youth. And this party he threw, like all of them do, eventually ended. But the way it ended should speak loudly with warning to our current pleasure-driven society.

Belshazzar's ancestor, King Nebuchadnezzar, had years earlier overthrown the holy city of Jerusalem. As part of the spoil, he had taken the sacred cups from the Lord's temple. Now on the night of this wild binge, Belshazzar, in his inebriated state, boldly called for those sacred cups that belonged to God. Into these he poured his intoxicating brew and began to boastfully toast his drink along with his orgy-loving friends.

Suddenly, as he was thus defying the God of heaven, the fingers of a man's hand appeared in the sight of all, high upon the palace wall, and wrote these words: *Mene, Tekel, Peres*. Of course, this strange event had a sobering effect on all present and quickly brought the festivities to a halt. The band stopped playing, the forks dropped, the loud, obnoxious laughter died down, and all stood uncomfortably numb before the words on the wall.

All eyes then turned toward the king. His face was pale with fear and his knees began to uncontrollably knock together. Soon his whole body was shivering with fright. Quickly, he called for all the wise men in his kingdom to tell him what the words meant, but none could decipher this mystical language. In desperation Belshazzar called for Daniel, that Hebrew captive who had years earlier been noted by Nebuchadnezzar for his wisdom. Daniel, who recorded this story for us in the fifth chapter of his book, knew the true God and by wisdom given from heaven quickly interpreted the message. In the hearing of all, Daniel began to speak to the king. "The first word [*Mene*] means that God has numbered the days of your kingdom and decided to bring it to an end. . . . The second word [*Tekel*] means that you have been weighed in the scales of heaven and found to be lacking the moral character you should have. The third word [*Peres*] means that your kingdom will be divided and given to the Medes and Persians" (Daniel 5:26-28).

So we might know that God means what He says, history faithfully records that on that very night the great city of Babylon was overtaken by the army of Darius the Mede. The young King Belshazzar never saw the light of the next day but was slain in his palace, his blood mixed with his drink. For him, the handwriting was on the wall—the party was over.

Similarly, dear friends, that same God has declared that the age-long party now going on in our world will one day come to an abrupt end at the second coming of Jesus Christ. The handwriting for this world is quickly appearing on the wall. Yet how few seem to sense the danger. We need not be surprised though. The Bible is full of indicators telling us that the world's end is very, very soon. Let us look at just a few.

An increase in knowledge

When I first began to believe in the second coming of Christ, I made a visit to my parents' home. There in the living room I began to enthusiastically tell my father that Jesus was about to come. I remember he looked at me with a gentle grin and said, "Keavin, when I was a boy, people were saying the same thing. Now I'm getting old. Someday you'll be old, too, and Jesus still will not have come." Somewhat shocked at his response, I then read him something I had been studying in the Bible. In reference to earth's last days, Daniel wrote, "There will also be an explosion of knowledge and many people will be traveling back and forth all over the world" (Daniel 12:4b).

Now, in the days when my dad's parents were young, people didn't travel like they do today. For the most part, they still relied upon the same mode of travel that had been used since the world began—animals. Amazingly, though, my grandparents lived to see men walk on the moon. People now travel "back and forth all over the world" just as thoughtlessly as they used to travel down to the local store. Never before in earth's recorded history has one generation witnessed such increase in technological knowledge.

Political and economic signs

The current state of world affairs provides suffi-
cient reason for most people to be concerned. Many
who don't even study Bible prophecy sense that something has gone wrong and that things cannot long
continue the way they are.

The Bible tells us that before the second coming
of Jesus, the nation's governments would begin to
counsel together in an attempt to solve the world's
problems. Over the last decade we have heard much
about a one-world government. Authoritative political
bodies such as the United Nations and the G7 now
represent the interest of many countries. Diverse nations now participate regularly in cooperative military
operations, are establishing new trade agreements
designed to create a global economy, and have banded
together to punish those countries who do not cooperate with their agendas. Our elected leaders in
Washington are no longer American politicians but
world politicians. Such global political arrangements
were predicted in the Bible as taking place near the
end of time.

When asked by His disciples what would be the
sign telling of His near return, Jesus said that "the
nations of earth will be in turmoil, and their leaders
will be perplexed" (Luke 21:25). I know of no greater
problem for our world leaders than the economic per-
plexities that now confront them.

America, though it is still an economic giant in
the world, is broke. Yet, economically speaking, we
baby-sit the world at no charge, except to ourselves.
World nations needing financial aid come to us because we are carrying around a credit card that seems
to have no limits. And with each passing year, while
our politicians spend time talking about balancing our

budget and cutting our national debt, we go deeper in the red. The United States' national debt increased from $900 billion to over $2 trillion during the decade of the 1980s.

The original Greek meaning of the word *perplexity* as used by Jesus means "no way out." Surely all can see that economically speaking we have reached that condition. Somewhere, somehow, this spending spree of our government, as well as American individuals, will come to an abrupt end.

Social signs

Nearly two thousand years ago the Christian apostle Paul wrote concerning the intense social problems that would exist in the world at the end of time. In reading what he wrote, one would think Paul was a current-day writer reporting on what he saw taking place around him. Especially in the last fifty years have these social symptoms of the end time been intensifying. Paul said, "You may as well know this . . . that in the last days it is going to be very difficult . . . for people will love only themselves and their money; they will be proud and boastful, sneering at God, disobedient to their parents, ungrateful to them, and thoroughly bad. They will be hardheaded and never give in to others; they will be constant liars and troublemakers and will think nothing of immorality. They will be rough and cruel, and sneer at those who try to be good. They will betray their friends; they will be hotheaded, puffed up with pride, and prefer good times to worshiping God. They will go to church, yes, but they won't really believe anything they hear" (2 Timothy 3:1-5, TLB).

Without question, such conditions are now a living reality in our world. For example, crime is ever on the increase. It wasn't many years ago that the criminals were behind bars while law abiding citizens strolled the parks and streets of our cities after dark. Now the scene is reversed. Citizens of cities the world over now lock themselves behind doors and barred windows at night while the thugs, rapists, and dope dealers occupy public grounds.

In 1940, the educators in America's public schools were surveyed concerning the worst behavioral problems exhibited by American youth. The survey response list was as follows: talking, chewing gum, making noise, running in the halls, getting out of turn in line, and improper clothing. In 1982, U.S. educators again were given the same survey for the same age group. What were the major reported problems of American youth only forty-two years later? Rape, robbery, assault, burglary, arson, bombings, murder, suicide, vandalism, absenteeism, drugs, alcohol, gang warfare, teenage pregnancies, abortion, and venereal disease.

But the problems of social relationships are not just with the youth in the schools. They begin with the adults at home. In times past when people got married, they did it with an intention to remain together for life. They entered the contract realizing that along with the honeymoon also came a life of responsibilities and commitments to fidelity. But today many, when choosing their life partner, seem to be thinking with their sexual anatomy rather than their brains. Consequently, when the initial infatuation begins to wear off and the pressures of married life sets in, couples young and old bail out of the marriage agreement. The Bible refers to this as "trucebreaking." As a result, more than half of the marriages in the United States end in divorce. And the end is not yet.

Another symptom of earth's last days that Paul mentioned to Timothy is the craze for pleasure. Today there is almost a constant drive by people to be entertained. Today media and big business entertainment is a twenty-four-hour-a-day industry. Small annual county fairs and the local zoos have mutated into Disney Worlds, Six Flags, and Sea Worlds. Keeping the mind occupied with pleasure has without question become the treatment of choice by this last generation in dealing with the stresses of modern-day living.

But no doubt the most disturbing evidence that our social fabric is being ripped apart is the low level of respect people now have for those in authority. This scourge can be witnessed daily at all levels of society, the saddest of all, being in the home. In referring to this social cancer of insubordination, the apostle Paul said we would be able to detect its earliest and most serious manifestation through children being disobedient to their parents.

Yes, it is a sad commentary that in many of today's homes children are the dominating factors. And what is even sadder is that many adults just laugh and comment about how cute these little rebels are. Then these little ones become nothing more than grown-up children who are determined to always have their own way. And as society fills up with such cursed people, the prospect for improvement of social relationships grows dim.

Religious signs

Another indicator that we are living in earth's last days is found in the religious world. Writing about our time, the apostle Paul said that people will be falsely religious. "Outwardly they'll look religious and be churchgoing folk, but they will not believe in the power of God to save them" (2 Timothy 3:5). Is this not an accurate description of many "so-called Christians" today? Only God knows how many people avoid the churches because there are so many hypocrites that fill them up. Though such an excuse is not justifiable before God, it is indeed a sad fact and will continue to be until the end.

The Bible warns us to be very cautious about the result of this religious hypocrisy, which is forecasted for these last days. Many religionists only *play* church, and the power of God's Spirit is not with them. Since it is God's Spirit manifested in the lives of His true followers that always wins converts to genuine Christianity, the Bible proclaims that these spirit-void churchgoers will one day seek to reform society's deteriorating morals by resorting to political legislation. It is an established historical pattern that when the church separates herself from the power of God, she turns to the power of persecution through the political state to win her converts. It was because of such a policy being followed in Europe in the 1600s that the Pilgrims set sail for America. And the Bible predicts that as we near this world's end, similar religious persecutions will revive.

Various signs foretelling the end

When we travel interstate highways, we usually gauge how close we are to our destination by road signs showing the number of miles left. Similarly, the Bible has listed many conditions that would exist just before the second coming of Christ to this earth. These social conditions serve as the signs of our times, telling us how close we are to the end.

Though there are too many to fully discuss, each deserves serious consideration. Following is a list of such conditions:

Increase in knowledge (Daniel 12:4)

People's obsession with accumulating wealth (James 5:3)

Great calls and movements for peace (1 Thessalonians 5:1-6)

Labor troubles (James 5:1-5)

Buildup of military armament (Joel 3:14, 9-12)

Man's ability to destroy the earth (Revelation 11:18)

False christs/prophets (Matthew 24:24)

People will be too busy (Luke 21:34)

Increase of bloody crimes (Ezekiel 7:23)

People making fun of the teaching of Christ's coming (2 Peter 3:3-5)

Turning to spiritualism (1 Timothy 4:1, 2)

Denial of Creation (2 Peter 3:3-6)

Religious skepticism (Luke 18:8)

Intemperance, uncontrollable physical diseases (Luke 17:29, 30; Ezekiel 16:49, 50)

Falling away from Bible truth (2 Timothy 4:1-4; Isaiah 30:8-10)

Disobedience of children to parents (2 Timothy 3:2)

Increase in arrogance (2 Timothy 3:7)

Foul, blasphemous speech (2 Timothy 3:1, 2)

Increase in display of sexual passions (2 Timothy 3:3)

Famines (Matthew 24:7)

Moral degeneracy and decline of spirituality (2 Timothy 3:1-5)

Unparalleled travel (Daniel 12:4)

Destructive earthquakes (Luke 21:11)

Disarmament talks (Isaiah 2:2-4)

Abounding lawlessness (Matthew 24:12; Isaiah 5:20, 24)

Unrest, upheaval among nations (Luke 21:25-27)

Craze for pleasure (2 Timothy 3:1-4)

Deceptive miracles (Revelation 16:14; 2 Corinthians 11:13-15)

Preaching of the gospel in all the world (Matthew 24:12-14; Revelation 14:6)

In this chapter we have examined information clearly indicating that the return of Christ and the end of the world are near.

Today, most Christians believe this but many predict that His second advent to earth will be a "secret" one in which He will rapture true believers out of this world. But does the Bible really support such a teaching? It clearly states that when Christ does appear the second time, it will not be a secret event (see Matthew 24:27). "Every eye shall see Him" (Revelation 1:7, KJV), and all the angels of heaven will be with Him (see Matthew 25:31). At that time those alive who have rejected His offer of grace will be slain by the brightness of His appearance (see 2 Thessalonians 2:8 and Jeremiah 25:33), and He will gather together His elect, both the dead whom He will resurrect, and the living, to be forever with Him (see 1 Thessalonians 4:16, 17 and Matthew 24:30, 31). But though His coming won't be a secret, it will be a surprise (see Matthew 24:44).

Even at the door

While on earth Jesus gave a simple parable that is more pertinent today than it was when He spoke it. After revealing some signs that would take place just before His return to earth, He said, "Now learn a lesson from a fig tree: When you see it put out new shoots and leaves, you know that spring is here. In the same way you can tell when the end is near, when it's right at the door" (Matthew 24:32, 33).

The fulfillment in our day of the things we have studied should be to us as the budding trees of spring. When we see those buds and blossoms in early April, we know what season is coming next. In like manner the Bible leaves us without excuse for not knowing what is soon to take place on old Planet Earth. Yet in the face of the evidence, most people will still choose to deny reality. But why?

It's like the story of the young boy and the cookie jar. While preparing supper, the boy's mother had to make a quick trip to the store for needed items. Her last instruction to her son was to save his appetite by not getting into the cookie jar while she was gone. But no sooner had she gone than the lad found himself going for the gusto. Yet in his mind he knew he could count on his mother coming back. If he could have honestly convinced himself that she wasn't, he could have enjoyed those cookies in peace. Instead, he stuffed his mouth while watching the door. Had he simply obeyed his mother, he would have been eagerly anticipating her return. But now the guilt of a violated conscience made him uneasy about any signs of her approach.

So it is today. Multitudes are uncomfortable concerning the teaching of Christ's imminent return because their hands are in the cookie jar of self-indulgence. "You only go around once in life," is the reasoning used, but we all know better. Living only for the moment always leaves empty results. The denial that Jesus is soon to come to put an end to our party-crazed planet is equivalent to a strong dose of Valium. Though it may provide temporary relief of our anxieties about the future, it doesn't change the fact that the willful, selfish behavior of our world is forcing Christ to soon come and end it. Just as it happened to King Belshazzar so long ago, soon this world will watch its party come to a close.

The only way we can excitedly anticipate the coming of Christ is to make our peace with God. Then we will not so much see the Second Coming as the end of this world but rather the beginning of an eternal life full of peace and happiness. That event is the only real hope this world has.

CHAPTER FOUR

Christians Who Break the Law

Thus far we have been discussing the role religion plays in our society. Having a great interest in these things myself, I enjoy discussing them with as many people as possible. I find the views and opinions as varied and numerous as the backgrounds of the people who share them. And yet, interwoven into this diverse patchwork of religious views, are common threads of ideology that, if carefully thought out and carried to their logical conclusion, really make no reasonable sense at all.

One such belief in the religious realm is the popular teaching that the Law of God, as is found written in the Ten Commandments, was done away with as a result of Christ's death on Calvary. This teaching is popular among modern Christians.

But whether we deem the law important or not, the Bible makes it clear that it is going to play a vital role in determining the destiny of individuals, churches, and nations. It will be over the issue of God's law that the last great battle between Christ and Satan will be fought upon this earth.

Lucifer began his rebellion in heaven by questioning the justice of God's law. God had established His heavenly government upon a system of law and order that perfectly provided for the happiness and contentment of all creatures. And it was God's law that guaranteed each inhabitant this perfect liberty, just as the Constitution of the United States grants each of its citizens their rights to a free and happy life. However, in time Lucifer came to dislike this order, so he rebelled against the established authority of God's law. And Lucifer has brought that same animosity toward God's law to this earth. He still maintains that the law of God cannot be obeyed and is only a hindrance and burden to true freedom. This is the lie which he has successfully perpetuated throughout the history of our world. Wherever this falsehood has been embraced, the inevitable results of lawlessness, chaos, and a total breakdown of social order has been witnessed.

The French Revolution

The most notorious example occurred in eighteenth-century France during what was called the French Revolution. France, by action of her legislature, rejected God's existence, thereby rejecting His law. Thus were the seeds of atheism planted, which would later yield a crop of great Communist empires in our own twentieth century.

The historical facts concerning the Revolution itself should teach us the far-reaching and ultimate results of disregarding God's law. With no moral law to govern by saying "You shall not murder" (Exodus 20:13, NKJV), the people soon turned on each other. The end result was "The Reign of Terror" in which thousands of France's sons and daughters, including the king himself, spilled their blood on the guillotine. And all this was due to the senseless decision of men and women to throw off the supposed binding restraints of God's moral code.

Modern revolution

So in our day many modern religionists have also cast aside the law of God through their doctrinal teachings. They have reasoned that since the Bible teaches we are saved by grace through faith in Christ alone and not by obedience to the Ten Commandments, we therefore are no longer under obligation to keep those laws. This they have done in an attempt to avoid legalism, which is the practice of trying to earn one's salvation by keeping or obeying God's law. But while legalism is to be feared, little do such religious teachers realize that they have tossed the baby out with the bath water. The results of dismissing the law as an unessential part of the gospel message can now be seen in the present condition of our society.

In reality, America and other so-called civilized nations are following a course similar to eighteenth-century France. Though the U.S. claims to be a Christian nation, isn't it really the sex idols of the magazines and movies; the sports heroes and music stars; and the industries promoting the consumption of alcohol, cigarettes, and food in gluttonous proportions that rule as gods over our society? We have just developed a "state-of-the-art" idolatry that allows for all our desires while at the same time we claim to believe in God. But the claims of God's law will one day bring us all to the test. It will eventually manifest the genuineness of our profession of Christianity.

Because God's law is communicated in the form of ten concise principles, many have difficulty relating to it. But it is really quite simple in its layout. (See Figure 4-1.)

THE TEN COMMANDMENTS
AS ORIGINALLY GIVEN BY GOD
(Exodus 20:3-17, KJV)

I

Thou shalt have no other gods before me.

II

Thou shalt not make unto thee any graven image, or any likeness of any thing that is in heaven above, or that is in the earth beneath, or that is in the water under the earth: Thou shalt not bow down thyself to them, nor serve them: for I the Lord thy God am a jealous God, visiting the iniquity of the fathers upon the children unto the third and fourth generation of them that hate me; and showing mercy unto thousands of them that love me, and keep my commandments.

III

Thou shalt not take the name of the Lord thy God in vain; for the Lord will not hold him guiltless that taketh his name in vain.

IV

Remember the sabbath day to keep it holy. Six days shalt thou labor, and do all thy work: but the seventh day is the sabbath of the Lord thy God: in it thou shalt not do any work, thou, nor thy son, nor thy daughter, thy manservant, nor thy maidservant, nor thy cattle, nor thy stranger that is within thy gates: For in six days the Lord made heaven and earth, the sea, and all that in them is, and rested the seventh day: wherefore the Lord blessed the sabbath day and hallowed it.

V

Honour thy father and thy mother: that thy days may be long upon the land which the Lord thy God giveth thee.

VI

Thou shalt not kill.

VII

Thou shalt not commit adultery.

VIII

Thou shalt not steal.

IX

Thou shalt not bear false witness against thy neighbour.

X

Thou shalt not covet thy neighbour's house, thou shalt not covet thy neighbour's wife, nor his manservant, nor his maidservant, nor his ox, nor his ass, nor any thing that is thy neighbour's.

Figure 4-1

Notice that the first four commandments instruct us in our relationship with God. The last six tell us how we should conduct ourselves in our interaction with our fellow humanity. In short, it is God's instruction to us as to how men and women should live in order to obtain true happiness. God Himself modeled such a life for us when He came to earth in the person of Jesus Christ. Christ was the living embodiment of God's law. The Old Testament Scriptures had said concerning God's law, "Your law is truth" and "all Your commandments are truth" (Psalm 119:142, 151, NKJV). Then when Jesus appeared as a real living man He said, "I am the ... truth" (John 14:6, NKJV). And near the close of His earthly life He stated, "I have kept my Father's commandments" (John 15:10, NKJV).

Such a life of obedience to God's commandments is what He desires for us. He knows that only a life of obedience can make us happy. "Righteousness exalts a nation" (Proverbs 14:34, NKJV). And "the work of righteousness will be peace" (Isaiah 32:17, NKJV). And what is righteousness? "For all Your commandments are righteousness" (Psalm 119:172, NKJV). Yes, the formula for true peace and happiness is found in the Ten Commandments. If these ten principles were but conscientiously carried out by the individual or the nation, it would increase peace, harmony, happiness, and prosperity.

On the other hand, disobedience to these principles will always bring its sure train of sorrow and misery. These results are as sure as that of violating the laws of gravity. Try jumping from a building a thousand times over and the result will ever be the same—you will crash every time. So it is when you violate God's law. Sometimes because we don't realize any immediate results of our disobedience, we think it makes no difference. But the Bible says, "You can be sure that you'll not be able to escape the consequences of your sins" (Numbers 32:23). Because "whatever a man sows, that he will also reap" (Galatians 6:7, NKJV). Though not immediately evident, sooner or later the results of our disobedience will appear to haunt us.

For example, can we not see the woe that has been brought upon our society because men and women so flippantly disregard the simple commandment forbidding adultery? Most often this act is committed in secret with no immediate consequences. But the violation of that one law has wrecked innumerable households and families and brought misery and heartache upon generations of offspring. Yes, it is vitally important that we understand exactly what role God's Ten Commandment law still plays in our lives. Only then will we be better equipped to make the right decisions and reap the desired results, thereby escaping the inevitable consequences of disobedience.

First, we need to understand that "for by the law is the knowledge of sin" (Romans 3:20, NKJV). Just as a mirror points out dirt on our faces, so the law points out our sins. Paul the apostle said, "I would not have known sin, except through the law" (Romans 7:7, NKJV). That is why the biblical definition of sin is "a breaking of God's law"(1 John 3:4, Phillips).

Now also notice that the Bible says, "Where there is no law, there is no transgression" (Romans 4:15, NKJV). Another translation puts it this way, "If there were no Law the question of sin would not arise" (Phillips). So you see, if you have no mirror, then you can more easily convince yourself that you have no dirt on your face. In other words, if we could do away with the law, then we wouldn't have to be faced with the fact that we are sinful. Here, dear friends, is the underlying motive as to why many professed Christians so eagerly teach and believe that the law has been done away with. They want to break the mirror instead of changing their lives.

Yet many of these same people sit in their churches and act dismayed at the degree of lawlessness and moral decline in our society. Today in America there is a murder every twenty-three minutes, a rape every six minutes, a robbery every fifty-eight seconds, a motor vehicle stolen every twenty-eight seconds, and a burglary every eight seconds! Lawlessness is so out of control that even *Time* magazine is now calling our country "America the Violent" (*Time*, 23 Aug., 1993). And yet when this nation has turned to the Christian churches, who are supposed to provide society with some barometer of morality, all that the churches have been able to tell them is that theologically speaking "there is no law." Let me say it plainly so the confusion may be swept away: To a great degree, the sins of this nation lay at the doorstep of the church.

But the problem of lawless behavior is not just confined to a society that is without Christ. It is also found in the very churches that profess to know Him. The divorce rate among professed Christians now rivals that of nonbelievers. In recent years we have all watched the moral demise of some of America's most popular preachers due to sexual immorality. Teenage daughters from Christian homes are getting pregnant without first getting married. Can we not see that the churches of this nation are but reaping what they have sown? And yet many self-righteously wonder why things are so bad and why so many in society want nothing to do with their churches and the God they promote. What the world really wants, and needs, is a living example of the highly ethical standard of living that exists when the commandments of God are carried out in life. And they don't so much want to hear it; they want to see it.

More and more church leaders are beginning to wake up to the fallacy of the teaching that the law has been done away with. In a 1989 sermon at the Carrier Dome in Syracuse, New York, the internationally popular evangelist Billy Graham stated, "Another thing that has never changed is God's moral law—the Ten Commandments. They have remained intact and God still requires obedience to them." Yes, many Christians are now realizing the vital role of the law in the gospel.

The Bible clearly states that "the law of the Lord is perfect, converting the soul" (Psalm 19:7, KJV). The way in which it converts us is that it shows us our sins and need for a change. It shows us our lost condition and convinces us that we need a Saviour. And everyone of us, with no exceptions, has a constant need to recognize our great sinfulness and continuing need for a Saviour. Where we have all failed is in fully realizing just how lost we are.

Do we really think that the drunkards and prostitutes in the slum districts of our society are lost, while so-called respectable church members, who benumb their brains with social drinks and who fantasize elicit sex with minds that have been programmed by television, are saved? No, my friends! Try as we may to deny it, God's standard of righteousness is much higher than that. It calls for our very thoughts to be brought into harmony with purity and truth (see 2 Corinthians 10:5). And God is no respecter of persons. If we enjoy playing around with and indulging even the thought of sin, it makes no difference whether we are a bum or a bishop; we come under the condemnation of God's holy law. And unless we recognize our true state and turn to Christ for His forgiving grace, we are lost. Not just lost for a moment but lost for eternity.

The law's role in the gospel

The Bible says, "The wages of sin [the breaking of God's law] is death" (Romans 6:23). Furthermore, "all have sinned and fall short of the glory of God" (Romans 3:23, NKJV). "There is none righteous [who has perfectly kept God's law], no, not one" (Romans 3:10, NKJV). So we are all in the same boat together. We have all sinned and deserve to die. Yet it is utterly amazing how people want to deny this fact and carry on as if they will live forever.

But the Bible means exactly what it says, that unless we see and confess our sinful, lost condition, we will die for eternity! Now who in their right mind really wants to die? Who wouldn't enjoy living forever without any sorrow and sickness, any financial troubles, or any burdensome toil? Only happiness, contentment, and carefree living throughout eternity. And yet we are not natural possessors of this peace when we come into this world. We receive no such inheritance from earthly parents. Only by accepting Christ as our personal Saviour can we begin to have such hope.

"Because of Adam's sin, a sinful and dying nature was passed on to everyone in the whole world" (Romans 5:12). God did not leave us helpless and hopeless but "showed His love for us while we were sinners—by nature, His enemies—in giving His Son to die for us." "Christ came to die for us while we were totally helpless and unable to do anything to become righteous" (Romans 5: 8, 6). Since Christ was sinless, He was like a vessel prepared to haul away contaminated material and could justifiably choose to receive and haul away the sins of mankind. But that toxic waste called sin had to be destroyed by death, and because Christ chose to bear it, He also had to die with it. That is why Jesus was nailed to the Cross and died. And by accepting His death in their place, mankind could be freed from guilt and condemnation and could then choose to live a life of right doing after the example of Christ. This can be summarized in one verse of scripture, "God made Christ to be sin for us, who knew no sin, so that He might pour Christ's righteousness into us so we could become more like God" (2 Corinthians 5:21).

But please note that it was not the law that was nailed to the Cross, but Christ. Christ didn't die to do away with the law but rather to do away with sin. Now by Christ's death forgiveness has been made available for all men, no matter how much they have sinned. The Bible thus tells us the condition of receiving this forgiveness: "If we confess our sins, He is faithful and just to forgive us our sins and to clean us up from all unrighteousness" (1 John 1:9).

This is the only real hope that exists in this dying world. Such a hope can only be realized by those who will stop excusing and justifying their lives of sin—who will humbly confess their sinfulness and their need. And the law of God is that moral indicator that speaks to our conscience, telling us that we have a need. Like a counselor who tells the alcoholic he has a drinking problem, so God's moral commandments point out to us our sin problem. Yet the alcoholic has no hope for recovery until he comes to the place where he will admit that the counselor is correct in the assessment of his problem. Thus it is with our experience of honestly looking into God's law and sincerely dealing with what it tells us about ourselves.

Many have interpreted verses such as Romans 6:14, "Sin shall not have dominion over you, for you are not under the law but under grace" (NKJV), to mean that we are no longer under obligation to keep the law. But the true interpretation is that we are no longer under the condemnation of the law's penalty, because we have by faith accepted Christ's sacrifice for us. By His death He has paid the penalty in behalf of those who will accept Him. "There is therefore now no condemnation to those who are in Christ Jesus" (Romans 8:1, NKJV).

But the fact that we have been saved by the grace of Christ in no way gives us license to disobey the law, for right after Paul stated in Romans 6:14 that "you are not under law, but under grace" (NKJV), he asks, "What then? Shall we sin (or break God's law) because we are not under law but under grace? Certainly not!" (Romans 6:15, NKJV). It must be understood that those saved by grace do not obey God's law in order to be saved, but they now obey God's law because they love Him for saving them. Their love for God is made manifest in their obedience to Him, for He says, "If you love Me, keep my commandments" (John 14:15, NKJV). It is through their obedience that their relationship with Christ is made known to others. "Now by this we know that we know Him, if we keep His commandments. He who says, 'I know Him,' and does not keep His commandments, is a liar, and the truth is not in him" (1 John 2:3, 4, NKJV). "For this is the love of God, that we keep His commandments. And His commandments are not burdensome" (1 John 5:3, NKJV). No, the keeping of the commandments are not a restrictive burden to the one who has been redeemed by grace. Obedience to these precepts is a joy and delight because they love God so much and they know that such behavior pleases Him.

Let's employ our common sense for a moment. Say I was driving my car in a forty-five miles per hour speed zone. But I'm driving sixty miles per hour, and a policeman pulls me over. He brings to my attention that I have broken the law and am deserving of a ticket. I plead with him for mercy, and he consents to let me go with no condemnation or consequences. I drive away free as a result of the officer's grace toward me. So now let me ask a question. If the next day I pass through that same forty-five-mile per hour zone driving sity miles per hour, will the same officer just wave and smile as I go by because I'm no longer under the law but have become a recipient of his grace? Or if he pulls me over again and tries to write me a ticket, will it do me any good to tell him that he can't ticket me today because I'm still under the grace of his pardon yesterday? Absurd, you say! Yet that is the same level of mentality being promoted by multitudes who are so quick to accept God's grace but want to ignore the still-binding claims of His law.

This is why many professing Christians, when they are confronted with their sins, quickly retort, "I was saved years ago, so now I'm under God's grace, not under His law." These false Christians excuse sin in their lives by presumptuously abusing God's grace.

But a real Christian's response is, "I delight to do your will O my God, and your law is within my heart" (Psalm 40:8, NKJV). They won't try to justify their wrong course but will humbly acknowledge their wrong and seek to bring their lives into harmony with the teachings of God's law.

Be not deceived

The erroneous teaching of "once saved, always saved" also can mislead people into believing they can go on sinning while claiming to be in a state of salvation. It teaches that once you have been truly saved by grace you can never again become lost, even if you sin. The Bible teaches no such concept. It clearly says, "When *a righteous man turns away from his righteousness and commits iniquity* and does the same abominable things that the wicked man does, shall he live? None of the righteous deeds which he has done shall be remembered: for the treachery of which he is guilty and the sin he has committed, *he shall die*" (Ezekiel 18:24, RSV, emphasis supplied).

The truth is that the gospel is more powerful than to leave the soul, whom it has saved, under the bondage of sinful living. Even Noah Webster defined saving "grace" as, "the divine influence of God in renewing the heart *and restraining from sin*" (*Noah Webster's Dictionary*, 1828 edition). Grace not only saves us from past sins but also empowers us to overcome sin in the future. The Bible says that Jesus came to "save His people from their sins" (Matthew 1:21, NKJV), not save them in their sins. The apostle Paul wrote, "Come to your right mind, and sin no more" (1 Corinthians 15:34, RSV). And John the beloved plainly states, "He who commits sin is of the devil. . . . No one born of God commits sin; for God's nature abides in him, and he cannot sin because he is born of God" (1 John 3:8, 9, RSV).

But while a life of victory over sin is the true experience of the Christian believer, we must guard against going to the far extreme of considering ourselves sinless. The apostle John also made clear the fact, "If we say that we have no sin, we deceive ourselves, and the truth is not in us" (1 John 1:8, NKJV). This apparent contradiction can be better understood when we realize the two ways in which God views sin.

First John 5:16 says that there is a "sin not unto death" and a "sin unto death." The sin that is "not unto death" is the sin that a Christian, who has already received pardon from Christ, may commit and not be aware that it is a sin before God. It is a sin of ignorance and is of a nature that God can justifiably cover with His grace, because "the times of ignorance God overlooked" (Acts 17:30, RSV). When the Christian is living up to all the light he has been given by God as to what is right or wrong, then "the blood of Jesus Christ His Son cleanses us from all sin" (1 John 1:7, NKJV). In such cases the Christian does not lose his right to eternal life because, even though he has sinned, it was done in ignorance, unintentionally, and it was "not unto death."

But when the Holy Spirit reveals to that same Christian that what he has been doing ignorantly is indeed a sin before God and then the Christian chooses to continue committing that sin, the sin is no longer one of ignorance but one of presumption. This type of sin is a "sin unto death," or a known sin. In other words, it is the willful commission of a sin that we already have been convicted is wrong. "Whoever knows what is right to do and fails to do it, for him it is sin" (James 4:17, RSV).

In God's view of justice, committing a *known sin* is an altogether different caliber of sin. If this is our case, then even though God's love for us doesn't change, the blood of Christ cannot justify us no matter how much we claim to be a Christian saved by His grace. Our condition is actually worse than it was before we ever came to experience forgiveness. The writer of Hebrews put it this way: "If we sin deliberately after receiving the knowledge of the truth, there no longer remains a sacrifice for sins, but a fearful prospect of judgment" (Hebrews 10:26, 27, RSV).

The one who willingly commits the "sin that is unto death" cannot possess life through grace because his sin has once again brought him or her into a state of spiritual death. Your only hope in such a situation is to turn from what you know to be wrong and to embrace Christ's forgiveness anew. We need to understand that this business of committing a willful sin is a serious one. It is more than just child's play with no lasting consequences. It is a matter of eternal life and death. Therefore, how serious should we be about it? If Christians only realized this, how carefully they would live their lives!

A common experience

Yet we also need to understand the long-suffering of God. There is the common experience, especially of the newborn Christian, of seeing a sin in the life and really desiring to do right by giving up the sin. Yet when we try to do what is right, somehow we end up doing what is wrong (see Romans 7:15-20). The key to victory here is that we continually confess the wrong and our weakness and earnestly seek God to give us the power to get the victory. When tempted, stop and think, "What would Jesus do if he were me?" and then strive with all your might to do it. When you fail, claim the promise in 1 John 1:9, accept His forgiveness, and try again. Don't give up or get discouraged, never excuse or justify the sin, and in due time God will cause you to hate that sin so much that you will turn from it with disgust. In allowing this to happen, God is strengthening our desire to do right and is developing in us a perfect hatred for our sins. This is a supernatural work that only God can do. It is God "who gives us the victory through our Lord Jesus Christ" (1 Corinthians 15:57, RSV).

So the ultimate plan of God concerning the work of His grace in our hearts is to bring our lives back into harmony with Him. This is the purpose of teaching us to obey His law. This is the covenant He has made with the Christian believers. Even though by birth our "mind is not in harmony with God's law" (Romans 8:7), God has promised that He will change the person who accepts His grace into his or her life by the power of the Holy Spirit. He says, "I will put my laws into their hearts, and write them on their minds" (Hebrews 10:16, NIV). Just as God in the days of old wrote His Ten Commandments on tables of stone, He now writes them in the hearts of men and women who will cooperate with Him.

As a result we will have a new life with new desires, new purposes, new ambitions, and new motives. The selfish become unselfish; the drunkard becomes sober; the slave to addictions is released from his bondage; the sexually impure become modest; the dishonest and greedy become the most upright and giving of all people; the proud become humble, while the know-it-alls become nonassuming. "Being then made free from sin, ye become servants of righteousness" (Romans 6:18, KJV). Their lives are radically changed, and through them the power of the gospel is given witness in the world. God lives out His law in their lives.

CHAPTER FIVE

The Real Trial
of the Century

For me it was a day that delivered shocking news.
I was driving home and had tuned into the hour's top
news stories. Out of Los Angeles had come the report that the police had just arrested O. J. Simpson
and charged him with murdering his former wife
Nicole and her male companion, Ronald Goldman.

Though I had long lost touch with the happenings
of Simpson's life (I stopped watching television over ten
years ago), the day's report had a strange impact on my
mind. It seemed to open the doors to memory's hallway.
"The Juice," as he was called, was a national hero. Many
were the Sunday afternoons I had spent watching
Simpson exhibit his extraordinary athletic abilities. I,
along with multitudes of others, thought they didn't make
them any better than O. J. Simpson. Yet, now he was
being charged with one of the goriest and most brutal
crimes of modern times. It was as though I took the news
personally.

Then, of course, ensued what was dubbed as the
"trial of the century." For months America was capti-
vated by the Simpson trial. And without question, that
trial and its result, Simpson's acquittal, will be the topic

of rehash for years to come.

But like everything else in this world, the hype surrounding the Simpson case was only another smoke screen used by the devil in an attempt to cover up the real trial of the century. He doesn't care how informed we were concerning the proceedings that took place in Judge Ito's courtroom, as long as we remain ignorant of the proceedings that are to determine our eternal destiny.

The Bible says that God "has fixed a day on which He will judge the whole world" (Acts 17:31, Phillips).

He also has appointed someone to be the judge and a standard by which everyone will be judged. The Judge will be Christ Himself. "For the Father judgeth no man, but hath committed all judgment unto the Son" (John 5:22, KJV). The standard by which we will be judged is God's law: "So speak ye, and do, as they that shall be judged by the law of liberty" (James 2:12, KJV).

Everything we've done in this life, including all those things we did in secret and thought we were getting away with must be judged by the law. All the deceptive business dealings, the infidelities to the marriage contract, all the lies told for the sake of convenience. It is "the day when God shall judge the secrets of men" (Romans 2:16, KJV). So the wise man Solomon counsels us, "Let us hear the conclusion of the whole matter: Fear God, and keep His commandments . . . for God will bring every work into judgment, with every secret thing, whether it is good or whether it is evil" (Ecclesiastes 12:13, 14, KJV).

Many have thought that Christ is not going to judge the world until He comes the second time. It will come as a rude awakening to them when they discover that by the time of His appearance the judgment will have already taken place! Speaking of the time when He does return to earth the second time, Jesus says, "behold, I am coming quickly, and *My reward is with Me, to give to every one according to his work"* (Revelation 22:12, NKJV, emphasis supplied). At that point there will be no appeal for anyone. Our decision for or against God will be final and irrevocable.

And who at that time will receive the reward of eternal life? Only those who through the grace of Christ learned how to obey His commandments. "Blessed are those who do His commandments, that they may have the right to the tree of life, and may enter through the gates into the city" (Revelation 22:14, NKJV).

Judged by the books

The Bible teaches that angels record all the thoughts and actions of men in documents or books that are to be brought forth and examined in this time of God's judgment. One of those books is the *Book of Remembrance* in which are recorded all the deeds of God's faithful servants (see Malachi 3:16). Also, there is the *Book of Life* in which the names of the faithful are recorded (see Revelation 20:12). Before the judgment now going on in heaven ends, everyone's life record will have been reviewed. Of those who pass this judgment God says, "I will not blot out his name from the Book of Life" (Revelation 3:5, NKJV). But those who fail to pass the judgment will not have their names written in that book of life but will suffer eternal destruction (see Revelation 20:15).

The Bible does not teach that there is a purgatory of second chances. God warns, "Man is destined to die once, and after that to face judgment" (Hebrews 9:27, NIV). Death only eternally seals the decisions we make in this life. At that point we have either made our peace with God or we haven't.

I often contemplate this when I'm in the presence of the terminally ill or the elderly. They instinctively seem to sense that they are soon to come face to face with the solemn event of dying, the time when the most important question will be, "What were the decisions made while living?"

On the other hand, I watch those who are still in the prime of their youth carelessly carrying on with life as though death is a long way off. And yet each morning, newspapers across this globe report that several more young people have met the grim reaper before they ever expected to. The sobering truth is that we don't know when death will knock at our door. But what we do know is that when it does come the time of probation granted us by God is over, and we must face final judgment.

In light of such weighty truth, how serious we should be about how we live! Court is in session. "The Lord is in His holy temple: let all the earth keep silence before Him" (Habakkuk 2:20, KJV). But instead of the silent reverence of humility during this solemn period of earth's judgment, God hears the buzz of excitement coming from the gambling casinos, the tatter of gunfire as people continue to take life from their fellow humans, the vulgar bickering between spouses and the miserable cries of their children, and the boastful words spoken by those who claim to know God but who really don't. He sees a whole nation that was more in tune and obsessed with the trial of O. J. Simpson than they are with what their own verdict will be before the heavenly tribunal. Oh, if we could but live beyond our five senses and view the things of reality as the Bible unveils them, what a different life most of us would live!

But there will be a people who, amid the corrupting elements of this present world, will understand their time of trial. And because of this, many of them have already begun making the necessary preparations for their legal defense in the justice halls of heaven. They will overcome their spiritual enemies and be found innocent of those sins they committed in this life and for which Satan, "the accuser of our brethren" (Revelation 12:10, KJV), claims that they should be destroyed. But how will they overcome? "And they overcame him by the blood of the Lamb" (Revelation 12:11, KJV).

Saved by the Lamb

The Bible says that "without the shedding of blood there is no forgiveness of sins" (Hebrews 9:22, RSV), and "the wages of sin is death" (Romans 6:23). Since blood is the most vital element of life, the shedding of it naturally results in death. And since it is sin that separates us from God, only through death, then, can we have remission of sins and be reconciled to God.

It has always been a lamb that has brought peace and reconciliation between God and man. After Adam sinned, God taught him about the destructiveness of sin by having him take the life of an innocent lamb. Adam had never witnessed death. Yet it was presented to him as the only way to forgiveness. So he took the life of that innocent little creature that had always looked at his master with eyes of love and trust. As Adam stood there in shock from the horror of the scene, the stain of crimson on his hand, he looked up and in agony cried out to God, "Is this what must happen to me because of my sin?" But God's answer came back with tender love that could melt the heart of the most hardened sinner, "No, my son, this is what must happen to Me because of your sin."

Adam then learned that the lamb was only figurative and pointed forward to that great Lamb who would one day have to be slaughtered in order to forgive the sins of humanity. That Lamb was none other than Jesus Christ—God Himself in human flesh. By becoming a human, He could yield up His blood and pay the debt of sin for the human race.

When that Lamb came to the earth, He came not to judge but to be judged on our account. Speaking of Him the gospel prophet Isaiah wrote, "He was oppressed and afflicted. He was mistreated and falsely accused, yet He bore it all without saying a thing. He was led as a lamb to the slaughter and as a sheep stands silent before its shearers, so He did not open His mouth. He was unjustly arrested, sentenced and led away to die. No one of His generation cared that He was cut off. He was nailed to the wood for sins of people who deserved to die. He was buried without honor as if He were a sinner" (Isaiah 53:7-9.

This takes us to another court scene. Not the one in Los Angeles or even the one in heaven but the one in Pilate's judgment hall. There we see Jesus of Nazareth being judged in our place. Even Pilate, a Roman governor, admitted, "I find no fault in him at all" (John 18:38, NKJV). But it was the time of the Passover, and the Jews had a custom with Roman authorities that a Jewish prisoner should be released to them at that time. So Pilate asked them if they wanted him to release Jesus unto them. "But the Jewish leaders said, 'Absolutely not! We want Barabbas [a convicted murderer] released, not Jesus!' " (John 18:40). So Barabbas was released while Jesus, though purely innocent of any wrong, was condemned to die by crucifixion. Barabbas, my friends, represents you and me.

So Jesus, the Lamb sent from God, died by giving up His blood to make a way of escape for us, even though, according to God's standard, we are guilty. Does that do anything to stir your heart, dear reader? The problem with us today is that we seem to have lost our value for life. Whereas Adam was unnerved by the death of a little lamb, today most American children have witnessed some 40,000 murders on television by the time they reach the age of eighteen. Nearly 24,000 people are murdered every year in the United States alone. No wonder death doesn't disturb us anymore.

But over the course of earth's centuries, the old story of a God who cares has broken the resistant hearts of the most callused sinners. It can do the same today. Before this life is over, many of the hardest hearts, even in this media-crazed and morally debased age, "will be filled with remorse because of their sins. They will see the One [Jesus] whom they crucified [by their lives of sin] and will weep and mourn as those who mourn the death of their only child" (Zechariah 12:10). The Holy Spirit will break through, and they will finally realize their unworthiness and come to appreciate the fact that Jesus died for them. They will accept the sacrifice of Calvary's victim and "having now been justified by His blood, we shall be saved from wrath through Him" (Romans 5:9, NKJV).

To sum up our whole discussion, Christ has already borne our condemnation if we will but accept it. But what more can He do for us if we reject this offer of freedom? If we reject Him, then we must die as payment for our own sins. Whether we want to accept it or try to ignore it, the fact is that this is the most important decision we will ever make.

What will you do with the Lamb? Will you wash your life-robe white in His blood, or will you someday hide from His wrath? (see Revelation 7:14 and Revelation 6:14-17). Will your sins make it into that heavenly sanctuary through confession before judgment closes? The problem of today is that there is too much profession of religious piety and not enough confession of sins.

Let us then go somewhere alone, with eyes that see by faith, and bare our selfish hearts to Him. Let's make an honest confession of our life of sin and acknowledge our need for Him to change our lives of disobedience. Then our names will be safely enrolled in the "Lamb's book of life." And when He comes the second time to execute the verdicts of justice, we will meet Him in peace.

CHAPTER SIX

Where Did
Sally Go?

It was a wet, wintry night as my parents and I made our way home from buying groceries. Suddenly we were alarmed by the passing of an ambulance. The sight and sound aroused my curiosity. *Where was it going?* I wondered. *Had there been a car wreck? Would I get to see it on the way home?* With a sense of wondering excitement, I told Dad to pick up the pace in pursuit. "Calm down," he said. "No use in us having a wreck chasing an ambulance." Around each curve and over every hill I watched for flashing lights piercing the dark night air.

My wait was not long, for we soon came upon one of the worst accidents my parents said they had ever seen. But this only increased my suspense, because the police quickly ushered us by before we could identify who was involved in the accident. Little did I know that the scene of that unforgettable night would touch my life in a way I would ever afterward remember.

Upon arriving at school the next morning, I found out that one of my best friends, Sally Howard, had been killed in that crash. Our whole school seemed to be in a state of shock. Within a few days, I attended the funeral services of my little fourth-grade playmate.

"Where did Sally go?" I asked.

"Oh, Sally went to heaven," someone replied.

I wondered how she got there. Even more, does everybody who dies go to heaven?

Such questions would puzzle me for years. As I grew older, I realized that I was not the only one with questions about death. Many fear death as the great unknown or harbor a false hope concerning what lies beyond the grave. Others simply try to think about it as little as possible.

Psychologists tell us that one of the first responses that many who have been diagnosed with a terminal illness go through is some form of denial that death will really come to them. But whether we deny it or try our hardest not to think about it, one thing is certain: We, along with everyone we hold dear in this life, will someday die. Indeed, it is a true saying that "any man can stop his life, but not one can stop his death."

Yet God would not have us be fearful of this mysterious experience. It is actually the world's ignorance on the subject that breeds its fear and uncertainty. Through the Bible, God plainly tells us what happens to people when they die. We can know the truth about this most mysterious topic.

The living soul

Because death is the disassembling of the human, we must first understand how man was put together. It is much easier to take something apart if you know how it was assembled. So we must go back to the time when we were created. "And the Lord God formed man of the dust of the ground, and breathed into his nostrils the breath of life; and man became a living soul" (Genesis 2:7, KJV). Here we have the recipe for a human being:

Dust of the ground + Breath of life = Living soul

This equation is as simple as one plus one equals two. Now, if you were to take one away, you would no longer have two but one. Similarly, if you take the breath of life away, which is the case at death, you would no longer have a living soul.

$$2 - 1 = 1$$
Living soul - Breath of life = Dust of ground

What exactly is the origin of these two simple components that make up the human structure? The Bible says that God "formed" man of the dust of the ground. Our forms are our physical bodies. The elements that compose our bodies are the same as are found in the soil. That is why we are nourished by nutrients from the soil through the plants we use for food.

The second component is the "breath of life," which came from God as He "breathed into his [Adam's] nostrils." This "breath of life" is also called our "spirit." Job said "all the while my breath is in me, and the spirit of God is in my nostrils" (Job 27:3, KJV). And the apostle James stated, "the body without the spirit is dead" (James 2:26, KJV). In the King James Bible, the marginal reading of "spirit" as used by James is "the breath."

What then happens to the body and spirit at the point of death? We are plainly told, "then shall the dust return to the earth as it was: and the spirit shall return unto God who gave it" (Ecclesiastes 12:7, KJV). Anyone who has gone through the experience of laying a loved one to rest knows all too well that the body (dust) is returned to the earth. In like manner, this same verse informs us that the spirit (breath of life) returns to God. The condition of our spirit at death is the same as it was before we came into existence. Just as man does not remember anything before he is born, so this spirit is not a living intelligence after death. The spirit or breath simply provides the spark of life to the body. Just as a battery cannot produce light without the components of the flashlight, so the spirit does not generate life apart from the body. Unless the body and spirit are together, it is impossible to have a living soul.

So then at death the unconscious spirit (breath) returns to God who gave it while the body goes to the grave. The original biblical meaning of the word *hell* is the grave. The dead are in their graves, whether righteous or evil, and are preserved there until a future resurrection. "Do not be amazed at this, for a time is coming when all who are in their graves will hear his [Christ's] voice and come out—those who have done good will rise to live, and those who have done evil will rise to be condemned" (John 5:28, 29, NIV).

Now notice that the Bible clearly teaches that man is completely unconscious and without knowledge or feeling at death. "The living know this at least, that they must die. But the dead know nothing, they have nothing for their labor, their very memory is forgotten, their love has vanished with their hate and jealousy, and they have no share now in anything that goes on in the world" (Ecclesiastes 9:5, 6, Moffat). "His spirit departs, he returns to his earth; in that very day his plans perish" (Psalm 146:4, NKJV).

Multitudes of popular preachers today tell us that when people die they ascend immediately to heaven to be with God, but the Bible declares, "the dead do not praise the Lord" (Psalm 115:17, NKJV). Would not the dead be praising God if they went to heaven when they died? Of course they would, but this is not the case according to the clearest scriptural teaching.

Contrary to popular belief, Adam forfeited immortality when he sinned. Immortality, for him, was conditional upon his obedience to his Creator. God had told him that through disobedience he would "surely die" (Genesis 2:17), but Satan told him just the opposite. "You will not surely die" (Genesis 3:4). Even though God later reaffirmed through His prophet that "the soul who sins shall die" (Ezekiel 18:20, NKJV), Satan has convinced nearly all Christendom that the soul is immortal and will never die.

Through Adam's sin, "death spread to all men" (Romans 5:12, NKJV). As a result, mankind no longer possessed immortality but, rather, is mortal. The Scriptures teach that only God is immortal (see 1 Timothy 6:16). Yet because of God's love for us, He "brought life and immortality to light through the gospel" (2 Timothy 1:10, NKJV). That is, He has made it possible for human beings to receive immortality again through accepting the gospel of Jesus. And while the apostle John points out that, by faith, we receive this gift of eternal life the moment we accept Jesus Christ as our Saviour (see 1 John 5:11-13), the actual bestowal of immortality will not take place until Christ returns. For the believer, death as we now know it is only a temporary, unconscious state of sleep. Then, at the Second Coming, "we shall not all sleep, but we shall all be changed—the dead shall be raised—and this mortal must put on immortality (see 1 Corinthians 15:51-54).

So then all the dead, whether righteous or unrighteous, unconsciously sleep in their graves while awaiting their rewards. Speaking of those who died possessing Christ as their Saviour, the apostle Paul tells us when they will be united with the Lord. It is at the second coming of Jesus Christ. "For the Lord Himself will come down from heaven, with a loud command, with the voice of the archangel and with the trumpet call of God, and the dead in Christ will rise first . . . And so we will be with the Lord forever (1 Thessalonians 4:16, 17, NIV).

This verse presents another question to those who believe that the dead go to be with the Lord as soon as they die. If the dead were already with the Lord, why would there need to be a future, end-time resurrection? The whole idea makes no sense but has gained popularity nonetheless.

Modern deception

It is upon this point that Satan is deceiving the inhabitants of the earth today! He has passed down to us, by religious tradition, the teaching that the soul continues to live after the spirit and the body separate. This unscriptural belief can easily be traced back to ancient pagan concepts. The Babylonians, Greeks, and Romans all taught that the dead ascended to a higher state of existence and often even worshiped their deceased as gods. Such false teaching is dangerous because it opens wide the door to spiritualism or communication with the dead. In the Old Testament, this practice was called necromancy and was strictly forbidden by God. A realization of the truth about the dead will help us avoid this delusion.

We are told that in the last days there will be "spirits of devils, working miracles" in an attempt to deceive men (see Revelation 16:14). One of these miracles already being performed is that of fallen evil angels appearing to the living, posing as those who have already died. With man already intrigued with the mysteries of death, this is proving to be a very powerful deception.

One example of this deception is the many reports claiming that the Virgin Mary is appearing and communicating with people in various parts of the earth. Nowhere does the Bible tell us that Mary ever rose from the dead and went to heaven. It says that of Jesus but not of Mary. Mary suffered the same fate as do all mortals at death. Elevating her to the status of a divine being after her death is following the pagan practice of creating gods out of deceased humans.

However, Jesus compared death to a state of unconscious sleep. One day news came to Him that a close friend named Lazarus was near death through sickness. A few days later Jesus said to His disciples, " 'Our friend Lazarus has fallen asleep, but I am going there to wake him up.' His disciples replied, 'Lord, if he sleeps he will get better.' Jesus had been speaking of his death, but His disciples thought He meant natural sleep. So then Jesus told them plainly, 'Lazarus is dead' " (John 11:11-14, NIV).

Upon arrival at the deceased's home, Lazarus's sister Martha, an early Christian believer, acknowledged her understanding of a future resurrection of the dead. When Jesus told her " 'your brother will rise again,' Martha answered, 'I know he will rise again in the resurrection of the last day' " (John 11:23, 24, NIV).

Then Jesus related to her the most important fact concerning death. He said to her, "I am the resurrection and the life" (John 11:25, NIV). When at His command they removed the door to Lazarus's tomb, Jesus exhibited the power of this claim by restoring life to Lazarus—an act that only the Lifegiver could perform.

Here is where our discussion should focus. Just as a patient undergoing surgery does not realize any expiration of time while under the anesthetic, so the time between the point of death and the resurrection is imperceptible. Time here is insignificant. But what is essential is that we know the Lifegiver if we ever hope to receive eternal life.

The Bible says the devil has "the power of death" (Hebrews 2:14). This is so because sin brought death, and Satan is the author of sin. He claims all who die as his. But Paul declared that Christ, by His death, opened the way by which He "might destroy him who holds the power of death—that is, the devil" (Hebrews 2:14, NIV). Some glad day sin and death will be no more. On that day all who accepted Christ as their personal Saviour and died believing in His promised power to resurrect them will be brought back from the land of the enemy.

What Jesus asked Martha He asks each of us to-day: " 'He who believes in Me, though he may die, he shall live. And whoever lives and believes in Me shall never die. Do you believe this?' " (John 11:25, 26, NKJV). Can you, dear reader, say with Martha, "Yes Lord, I believe that you are the Christ, the Son of God, who is to come into the world" (John 11:27, NKJV)?

Hope in death can be discovered only through hope in Christ. If we possess this kind of faith in the Lifegiver, then we have truly solved the mystery of death that baffles the world. On the resurrection day, it will be heard from our lips, "Where now, O death, is your victory; where now is your stinging power?" (1 Corinthians 15:55, Phillips).

CHAPTER SEVEN

Flickering Firelight

Winter was always a time of real trial for me as a boy. The bad weather limited what one could do for fun outside and seemed to make the already dreaded farm chores even more unbearable. And even staying warm in our uninsulated old farmhouse often proved to be a real challenge.

In order to save heat, my parents would shut off the sleeping rooms from the central part of the house where the old coal furnace was. Needless to say, this made for some very frigid experiences as my brother and I went to bed at night. To help the situation, my father sometimes went to our room and started a fire in the little wall grate.

Those simple little fires had an enormous impact upon my mind. I remember running across the cold floor and diving in under the multiple layers of quilts and blankets. Then my mother, after tucking my brother and me in, would turn off the light as she left the room. As I lay on my back in the still darkness, the only stimulus to the senses was the crackling of the coals and the light from the fire flickering on the walls and ceiling.

It was in this setting that I first began to contemplate a place called hell. I had often heard preachers try to portray the terrifying conditions of its burning caverns and the dreadful agony of its hopeless inhabitants.

Could the preachers be right? Was there really a place in the earth's core where people were unmercifully tormented with fire throughout eternity? The special effects of my illuminated bedroom seemed to suggest there was. My young mind would often ponder such things to the point that sometimes it seemed as though the devil himself was in my room. This mental torture would often freeze me so badly with fright that I dared not move a muscle lest hell's captain grab me and take me there. I wished I could run to some part of the house that had light.

The subject of hell has spooked the members of the human race for centuries. Many have tried to gain heaven only out of fear of hell. Others, in convincing themselves that there is no hell, have come to believe there is no heaven either. Though the Bible clearly speaks of both, generations of honest-hearted Christians have had an erroneous view of hell that is not found in the Bible.

The idea of hell as a place with dark caverns, fire and brimstone, and souls eternally writhing in agony is simply another part of Satan's well-devised strategy to pervert man's understanding of the marvelous character of God. And once again this false teaching has only gained a stronghold in religious realms through ignorance of what the Bible really says. Multitudes of popular preachers have effectively used this powerful, deceptive doctrine as a tool to move people off the benches of secular society and into the pews of their churches. But through such a teaching God's real character has been terribly perverted. It has caused men and women to look upon Him as One who satisfies His thirst for revenge by tormenting souls forever.

A relationship of love

We should maintain a certain degree of respect and reverential fear toward God. It is a biblical fact that God will one day have no other choice but to destroy those who have slighted His merciful offer of salvation and selfishly chosen to live as if they had to give account to no one. Jesus put it this way, "Do not fear those who kill the body but cannot kill the soul. But rather fear Him who is able to destroy both soul and body in hell" (Matthew 10:28, NKJV). But while fear may give us some motivation, God wants us to learn to obey Him through love, not fear. He said, "If you love me, keep my commandments" (John 14:15, NKJV).

The relationship God is hoping for, one built upon the principle of love, can better be understood by those of us who are parents. There are two primary ways of extracting obedience from our children—by threatening them with consequences or by gaining their love and respect. I ask, which will make us happier as parents, to have the child obey because we've given the ultimatum or to know that our offspring are obeying, maybe even when they don't feel like it, because of their love for us? The quality of the motivation for obedience here is incomparable!

It is no different in our relationship with God. He doesn't warn us about the consequences of disobedience just to scare us into serving Him. He warns us because He loves us and doesn't want us to suffer those consequences. Like a parent who warns a young child not to touch a red-hot stove, God doesn't want to see harm come to any of His creatures.

As for eternally securing our obedience, the Lord knows that the only lasting motivation will be our love for Him. That is why He sent Jesus here to reveal His character and also why the devil has been so determined to misrepresent Him to us. Satan knows that if we ever come to realize that God is a real, delightful person, that He is extremely fascinating, easy to approach, and One who loves us and craves to receive our affections, then we would actually feel relaxed in His presence and fall in love with Him. Love begets a desire to please the one we love. So, when we learn to love God, it will be natural to obey Him, just as lovers naturally want to do what pleases their beloved.

Dear friends, Satan is jealous for your affections and would like nothing more than to cause you to fear and hate the One whom it is your privilege to trust and adore. Therefore he exaggerates what God will do to you if you refuse to obey Him. The doctrine of eternal burning hell is that exaggerated lie. It is actually a twin sister to the deceptive teaching that our souls continue to live after we die. It is this false view of death, which I exposed in the preceding chapter, that actually gives credence to the heresy of an eternally-burning hell. While many hope their loved ones went to heaven when they died, there is always the possibility they went the other direction. Many who have outlived their friends and family have been driven to the brink of insanity and hostility toward God with the thought that their loved ones may be burning in hell. Thus the devil's sole purpose of this dragnet of deception is to turn us away from the only One who offers us any hope, the Lord Jesus Christ.

So let us now uncover what the Bible really says about the fate of the wicked.

It has actually been a misapplication of words and

phrases that has resulted in the teaching of an eternally-burning hell. When describing the fate of the unrighteous, the Bible speaks of "eternal fire" (Jude 7, NKJV), a "fire that never shall be quenched" (Mark 9:43, NKJV); of "everlasting punishment" (Matthew 25:46, NKJV), and "everlasting destruction" (2 Thessalonians 1:9, NKJV); and of "the smoke of their torment ascends forever and ever" (see Revelation 14:11). As a result, generations of sincere Christians have concluded that unrepentant sinners will burn in hell "forever and ever"—throughout eternity. Yet, a closer investigation of the Bible's use of these terms does not yield such a conclusion.

We must be careful where we place the emphasis of such words as "eternal" and "everlasting." Most have used it so as to modify the word "fire." But the ultimate reward of the unsaved is not fire, but death. As it is written, "The wages of sin is death" (Romans 6:23). Here is where the emphasis needs to be placed. The consummating result of "eternal fire" is "eternal death." The fire is simply the means by which a person will be brought to their final, eternal state of death, spoken of in the Bible as the "second death" (see Revelation 21:8).

Likewise, when the Bible speaks of "everlasting punishment" or "everlasting destruction," it is using the adjective "everlasting" to modify the words "punishment" and "destruction." It doesn't say that the punishing or destroying by fire goes on for eternity. Rather the "punishment" or "destruction," which is the death resulting from the fire, is what is eternal. Revelation 21:8 makes clear that fire is the element used to bring the sinners to a final, eternal death: "But the cowardly, the unbelieving, the vile, the murderers, the sexually immoral, those who practice magic acts, the idolaters and all liars—their place will be in the fiery lake of burning sulfur. This is the second death" (NIV).

This concept of eternal death can be better understood when contrasted with eternal life. When one inherits eternal life, he or she will continue to live forever and ever throughout eternity. On the other hand, eternal death is exactly the opposite—an unconscious state of nonexistence throughout all eternity. It is an eternal separation from God, the very source of all life power. If the lost were consciously burning in hell for eternity, then the wages of their sins would not be death but rather an inferior, agonizing form of eternal life. The Bible simply does not teach such a concept.

It is the same old lie Satan told Eve in the garden, that if you sin, "you will not surely die." Now he tells man that the soul who chooses sin shall not die but continue to live while burning eternally. But the Bible has plainly said, "The soul who sins . . . will die" (Ezekiel 18:20, NIV). And when the Bible says that it will die, that is exactly what it means. Think about it, how can a soul be dead if it is alive and burning forever? Such a teaching simply doesn't square up with the Bible or even simple human logic.

True, the Bible speaks of an "eternal fire," but we must closely examine the nature of this fire. The phrase is found in Jude, verse seven, where it says, "Even as Sodom and Gomorrah . . . are set forth for an example, suffering the vengeance of eternal fire" (KJV). But what was the end result of those cities that serve as examples suffering "the vengeance of eternal fire?" What actually happened to Sodom and Gomorrah when they were burned by eternal fire? Are they still burning with eternal fire today? Of course not.

The Bible tells us what happened to them, "Turning the cities of Sodom and Gomorrah to ashes he condemned them to extinction and made them an example to those who were to be ungodly" (2 Peter 2:6, RSV). From this account there is no doubt what the end result of the "eternal fire" was for Sodom and Gomorrah. It turned them into "ashes" and made them literally extinct. And they are the biblical example of what will be the final fate of the ungodly. They, too, will ultimately be reduced to ashes.

God, speaking through His prophet Malachi to those who will inherit eternal life, says, "Behold, the day comes, burning like an oven, when all the arrogant and all evildoers will be stubble; the day that comes shall burn them up, says the Lord of hosts, so that it will leave them neither root nor branch. But for you who fear my name the sun of righteousness shall rise. . . . And you shall tread down the wicked, for they will be ashes under the soles of your feet, on the day when I act, says the Lord of hosts" (Malachi 4:1-3, RSV).

This is the biblical truth concerning the final end of sin and sinners. The root spoken of here is the originator of sin, the fallen angel Satan. In speaking to him God also foretold his final end, "I brought forth fire from the midst of you; it consumed you, and I turned you to ashes upon the earth in the sight of all who saw you . . . you have come to a dreadful end and shall be no more forever" (Ezekiel 28:18, RSV).

Notice that as a result of fire Satan "shall be no more forever." That is, he passes into extinction. This is eternal death, an eternal nonexistence. And this will be the fate of all humans who choose to hang onto sin. They can never spend eternity with God because sin cannot withstand the immediate presence of God.

To sin, God is a consuming fire (see Hebrews 12:29).

This whole lesson can be better understood by the following illustration. If you were to take a book and show it to a large group of people, all could and would identify the object as a book. But if you were to then set the book on fire until it completely burned up, you would be left with only a small pile of ashes. Then people would not identify the refuse as a book. And why? Because the book no longer exists. And what's more, it will never be a book again throughout eternity because it has been eternally burned up! But note that the fire itself burned only as long as there was anything left to consume. Once the book's substance was completely incinerated, the fire died out.

When asked by someone "what happened to the book?" we could reply that "it all went up in smoke." That's exactly what the Bible says about the destruction of the wicked, "The wicked shall perish, and the enemies of the Lord . . . they shall consume; into smoke shall they consume away [vanish]" (Psalm 37:20, KJV; see also Isaiah 51:6). So we see that not only will the wicked be reduced to ashes but they will also be consumed into smoke and vanish away, just like the book.

Yet not withstanding such logical and clear scriptural evidence, some who want to hang onto the idea that souls eternally burn in hell will quote Revelation 14:11. There, speaking of the destruction of the wicked, it states that "the smoke of their torment ascendeth up forever and ever" (KJV). It might seem that since the smoke ascends "forever and ever," then the fire must burn forever and ever. But once again we must pay closer attention as to how the word "forever" is used in Scripture.

Scripturally speaking, *forever* indicates the period

of time for which something will last. In the case of the prophet Samuel's tenure of service in the Lord's temple, *forever* referred to the length of Samuel's life. When considering the dedication of her son to that service, Samuel's mother, Hannah, said, "I will bring him, that he may appear in the presence of the Lord, and abide there forever" (1 Samuel 1:22, RSV). She went on to say, "Therefore I have lent him to the Lord; as long as he lives he is lent to the Lord" (1 Samuel 1:28, RSV). Thus we see that Samuel's period of service in the temple, the length of which was considered "forever," was actually as long as he lived.

Exodus 21:6, when speaking of a slave's lifelong time of service to his master, says "he shall serve him *forever*" (KJV). In other words, as long as the slave lives, he shall serve his master. In like manner of those who shall inherit eternal life we are told, "They shall reign forever and ever" (see Revelation 22:5). They will reign for as long as they live, which in this case will literally be "forever," throughout the ceaseless ages of eternity. But when we refer to the smoke of the wicked's torment ascending "forever and ever," we must understand that their smoke will ascend only as long as their life shall last, or "forever." Simply stated, they will burn with smoke until they are finally reduced to ashes and there is nothing left to burn, as was our example with the book.

Others maintain that Jesus spoke of a "fire that can never be quenched" (see Mark 9:43, 45). But was He referring to a fire that would never go out, one that would continue to burn for eternity?

Prophesying the destruction of Jerusalem with fire, Jeremiah said, "Then I will kindle a fire in its gates, and it shall devour the palaces of Jerusalem and shall not be quenched" (Jeremiah 17:27, RSV). That prophesied event actually took place when the Babylonian armies came against Jerusalem in 587 B. C., but we know the city's gates are not still burning. The "unquenchable" characteristic of such fire is that no one can possibly put it out while there is anything left to burn. But once all that can be burned has been burned, then the fire extinguishes itself for lack of any combustible fuel. So will it be when the wicked are reduced to ashes. No power apart from God will be able to put those flames out while they are devouring those who rejected eternal life. But after it has done its work, the "unquenchable" fire will go out on its own.

Doesn't it all make sense? Only a god with the heart of a devil could derive satisfaction through seeing His creation suffer in extreme agony throughout eternity. I would like to ask those who promote such theology, How would it appease your righteous souls if it were one of your own children who thus burned? Could you honestly enjoy life in heaven if you knew that such an eternal holocaust was taking place? Well, neither could God!

Though He is indeed just in dealing with the crimes of the wicked, He is also merciful, even when He executes justice. And only a God of mercy could devise such a practical plan cleansing the world of sin. Rather than tormenting sinners for eternity, He will simply burn them up until they no longer exist. Yet how comforting to know that even in this ultimate reward for sinners, which is eternal death, there will be no perpetual pain, suffering, torment, or agony.

With all this focus on punishment and destruction, it's easy to see why it is difficult for us to obtain a right concept of a loving God. Many say, "If God is really a God of love, then why will He destroy sinners?" But we must understand that God must destroy sin or else the misery of broken homes, disease and suffering, war, and death, would forever continue. He realizes that just one

creature who willingly cherishes and holds onto sin
threatens to destroy the peace, happiness, and harmony
of the entire universe. We must never forget that the
whole sin problem began in the heart of only one creature, Lucifer. So the fact that people must be destroyed
along with sin is not due to God's choice but rather results from their unwillingness to give up sin and separate
themselves from it. While God hates the sin, His eternal
love for sinners was made clear through the apostle Paul
when he wrote, "God shows His love for us in that while
we were yet sinners Christ died for us" (Romans 5:8,
RSV). Only One with a heaven-born love would die for
those who hate Him. Yet this is what Christ, our God,
did for us. And as a result of His death, we sinners, who
were in total bondage to Satan, are now free to choose
Christ instead of sin. If we will but do this, then we will
live eternally. This is God's desire for us—that we will
choose life instead of death. "As I live, says the Lord
God, I have no pleasure in the death of the wicked, but
that the wicked turn from his way and live; turn back,
turn back from your evil ways; for why will you die?"
(Ezekiel 33:11, RSV).

Those who are currently choosing a life of sin,
can you hear God with the intense concern of a loving
father calling to your heart, "turn back, turn back"?
The truth and sum of the whole matter is that where
we spend eternity will depend on how we answer the
God who thus loves us. Will we live throughout eternity with Him and all those who chose Him? Or will
we be burned into eternal nonexistence? God wants
us to be saved. But He leaves the decision to us.

CHAPTER EIGHT

The Day the World Forgot

I awoke to a brisk, sunny autumn morning in Knoxville, Tennessee. It was Saturday, and a big day for the University of Tennessee football fans. Football had long been one of my favorite sports, and a stadium that held 100,000 spectators made the event even more thrilling.

But today was going to be an altogether different day for me; a day such as I had never known before. So I quickly got ready, joined my wife for breakfast, and then we drove into town. As we hit the main street that led to the stadium, there was very little traffic. Usually one trying to get down Kingston Pike on a Saturday when the Volunteers were playing could anticipate a long wait. But on this day we had no problem because we were early—early for the game, that is, but right on time for where we were going. For, you see, on this Saturday morning we were going to church. No, not for a wedding or a funeral but for a regular weekly worship service.

Now normally the doors of the church would be all locked up on a Saturday morning, but not the church we were to attend that day. The people who met there were known as Sabbath keepers. Strange sounding concept, you say? People going to church on Saturday rather than Sunday? Well, it might not have been so unusual if they had been Jews, but they weren't—they were Christians.

If all this seems foreign to you, then join my club. I had been living for twenty-five years and had never before heard of it. Yet my inquisitive side wanted to investigate the whole matter. What I discovered I would like to share.

I had always believed that Sunday was the day Christians were commanded by God to go to church for worship. But when I began earnestly searching the Bible for evidence of this belief, much to my surprise, there was none. Instead, I found that the Bible most explicitly teaches that Saturday, the seventh day of the week, is the biblical day of worship for Christians. One of the Ten Commandments says, "Remember the Sabbath day, to keep it holy. Six days you shall labor and do all your work, but the seventh day is the Sabbath of the LORD your God" (Exodus 20:8, NKJV). You are probably asking yourself, "If this is true, then why does the majority of the Christian world worship on Sunday?" That we will clearly answer, but first I would like to show you the substantial proof that had led my wife and me to church that autumn Saturday morning.

Evidence from dictionaries and encyclopedias

Looking at a calendar might be enough to persuade most people that Saturday is the seventh day of the week. But not me. I had to look it up in dictionaries and encyclopedias. Here's a sampling of what I found:

Webster's New Twentieth Century Dictionary, 2nd Edition, unabridged (1973): "Seventh day, Saturday, the seventh day of the week."

World Book Encyclopedia (1975): "Sabbath" . . . "It comes on Saturday, the seventh day of the week."

Encyclopedia Americana (1973): "Sabbath, the weekly day of rest and religious observance. The term is . . . denoting the seventh day of the week, or Saturday."

Colliers Encyclopedia (1973): "Sabbath—Biblically the seventh day of the week, a day of rest and joy consecrated to the Lord."

In addition to this, I soon learned that over 140 languages around the world use the word *Sabbath* when referring to the seventh day of the week (e.g., the Spanish word for Saturday is *sabado*).

Scriptural evidence

The greatest pool of evidence that establishes Saturday as the Sabbath is found in the Bible itself. From the time this earth was created until it ends, and even after it has been created anew, the Scriptures substantiate the seventh day as the true Sabbath for religious worship.

Many people think God gave the Sabbath only to the Jews and that Christians are commanded to keep Sunday. In actuality, God gave the Sabbath to the entire human race at the time of Creation, some twenty-three hundred years before the first Jew existed (see Genesis 2:2, 3). Jesus confirmed this when He said, "the Sabbath was made for man" (Mark 2:27, KJV). Notice that He didn't say the Sabbath was made "for the Jew."

The Bible also tells us that the Lord was leading His people to observe the seventh day even before He gave them the Ten Commandments at Mount Sinai (see Exodus 16). When He did finally deliver the Ten Commandment law, which contained instructions on

Sabbath observance, He wrote it down in stone. Stone is an enduring material that does not change or give way over time. When we want to express that something is final and irrevocable, we often say, "You can write it down in stone." Likewise, the Sabbath commandment, along with the other nine, was to be perpetual throughout all generations.

These commandments were the only part of the entire Bible that God trusted no man to write but penned them Himself (see Exodus 31:18). And regarding the fourth commandment, the one that calls for the religious observance of Saturday, God said "Remember the Sabbath day, to keep it holy" (Exodus 20:8, NKJV). What is the only reason why we tell someone to "remember" something? It is because we think they might have a tendency to forget. Was God legitimate in His concern that the human race might forget "the Sabbath day, to keep it holy"?

The Scriptures clearly teach that Jesus, the Creator who had created the seventh-day Sabbath, kept that day as His day of worship while a man upon earth. "So He [Jesus] came to Nazareth, where He had been brought up. And as His custom was, He went into the synagogue on the Sabbath day, and stood up to read" (Luke 4:16, NKJV).

Christ's followers were honoring the seventh-day Sabbath at the time of His crucifixion (see Luke 23:52-56). Jesus had also inferred that the early Christians would be regarding the Sabbath day as sacred when they would have to flee Jerusalem as it was about to be destroyed by the Roman armies. He forewarned them to "pray that your flight may not be in winter or on the Sabbath" (Matthew 24:20, NKJV). This event actually took place in A. D. 70, some years after Jesus had ascended to heaven and nearly 40 years after the establishment of the Christian church. And still Jesus expressed concern that their fleeing Jerusalem not interfere with their Sabbath observance.

The Bible also says that the great Christian apostle Paul kept the seventh-day Sabbath as a day of religious observance (see Acts 18:4). Even pagan Gentiles who were interested in hearing the Word of God requested that Paul come preach to them on the Sabbath day (see Acts 13:42-44). And the book of Hebrews, a letter written to New Testament Christians, gives straightforward counsel regarding observance of the seventh-day Sabbath. It says, "There remains a Sabbath rest for the people of God; for anyone who enters God's rest also rests from his own work, just as God did from His" (Hebrews 4:9, 10, NIV). And what day did God rest from His labors of creating this world? "And on the seventh-day God rested from all His work" (Hebrews 4:4, NIV; see also Genesis 2:2, 3).

Notwithstanding the insistence of some who say the Bible teaches that the early Christians were keeping Sunday, the proof of that claim is simply nowhere to be found in the Scriptures. As a matter of fact, the first day of the week, as it is called in the Bible, is only mentioned nine times in the entire Scriptures. Not one of those texts proclaim Sunday to be sacred or teach that it was to ever replace the seventh day. Yet people presumptuously take some of these texts out of their context and try to make them say more than they do.

The apostle John also acknowledged the seventh-day Sabbath when he wrote, "I was in the spirit on the Lord's day" (Revelation 1:10, KJV). Today nearly the entire Christian world has been taught that "the Lord's day" is Sunday. But is that what the Bible teaches? Did the Lord lay claim to any day as being His? Indeed He did! In the Old Testament the Lord claimed "the Sabbath" as "my holy day" (see Isaiah 58:13). And in the New Testament it is recorded three times that the Lord Jesus laid a personal claim to the Sabbath. He said, "The Son of Man is Lord of the Sabbath" (Luke 6:5, NIV; see also Matthew 12:8 and Mark 2:28). Which day did the Lord say He was Lord of? The Sabbath day! And the same Lord says, "I am the Lord, I do not change" (Malachi 3:6, NKJV). "Jesus Christ is the same yesterday, today, and forever" (Hebrews 13:8, NKJV). Yes, the same day Jesus claimed yesterday, He still claims today. It was Saturday, the seventh day, not Sunday, that John was referring to when he mentioned "the Lord's Day."

John also saw in prophetic vision that right down in the last days of earth's history there would be people keeping God's commandments (see Revelation 14:12). Since one of those commandments teaches the observance of the seventh day as a day of rest, then obviously these people will be keeping the Sabbath. The last book of the Bible says, "Blessed are these who do His commandments, that they may have the right to the tree of life, and may enter in through the gates into the city" (Revelation 22:14, NKJV).

And lastly, when speaking of the experience of those who finally see the eternal world, the Bible says that even there they will be keeping the Sabbath. Speaking of the time when this present earth has passed and the new earth is created, Isaiah said, "From one New Moon to another, and from one Sabbath to another, all flesh shall come to worship before Me,' says the Lord" (Isaiah 66:23).

So now notice the continuity of the Bible's teaching regarding the Sabbath. God gave His seventh-day Sabbath to man at Creation; the Jews kept it; Jesus kept it;

Paul, John, and the early Jewish and Gentile Christians kept it; Revelation predicts that many Christians in the final days of earth's history will be keeping it; and finally, God's people who live in the new earth will come to worship God on His original seventh-day Sabbath.

Evidence from Bible scholars

Yes, to the honest seeker of truth there is no doubt as to what the Bible teaches about the Sabbath: It is Saturday, not Sunday. But this fact is not just acknowledged by those Christians who are presently keeping the Saturday Sabbath as their day of rest and worship. This truth has been verified by Bible scholars from nearly every major Sunday-keeping denomination. Consider what these Bible scholars have said.

Evangelicals

Christianity Today, a leading evangelical journal: "There is nothing in Scripture that requires us to keep Sunday rather than Saturday as a holy day." Dr. Harold Lindsell, editor, in his lead editorial, 5 November 1976.

Baptist

"There was and is a commandment to keep holy the Sabbath day, but that Sabbath day was not Sunday. There is no scriptural evidence of the change of the Sabbath institution from the seventh to the first day of the week." Dr. Edward Hiscox, author of *The Manual of Baptist Churches* from the *New York Examiner*, 16 November 1893.

Lutheran

"There is no command in the Bible to keep Sunday as a day of rest. Why do we keep Sunday? The seventh day is not the first." Pastor H. Bilenberg, 20 June 1933.

Methodist

"If the New Testament silence on any subject proves that a matter is unimportant, then the Christian emphasis on the observance of Sunday is really a mistake. Nowhere does the Bible tell us to observe Sunday. Nowhere does it say that Saturday Sabbath keeping is wrong." *Methodist Epworth Herald*, Editorial, 21 July 1923.

Christian (The Disciples of Christ)

"There is not testimony in all the oracles of Heaven that the Sabbath was changed or that Sunday came in place of the Sabbath." Alexander Campbell, *Washington Pennsylvania Reporter*, 8 October 1821.

Presbyterian

"Some have tried to build the observance of Sunday upon apostolic command, whereas, the apostles gave no such command on the matter at all. . . . The truth is, as soon as we appeal . . . to the Bible the Sabbatarians have the best of the argument." *The Christian at Work*, an editorial.

Episcopalians

*"The Bible com*mandment says on the seventh day thou shalt rest. That is Saturday. Nowhere in the Bible is it laid down that worship should be done on Sunday." Newspaper Article in *Toronto Daily Star* for 26 October 1949—Reverend Philip Carrington—headline read, "Clergy Say That Sunday Keeping Not In The Bible."

Church of God

"In regard to the matter of what day we ought to keep holy, I will say that I hereby offer you or anyone else Five Thousand Dollars ($5,000.00) if they will produce ONE TEXT from the New Testament which says that we ought to keep the first day of the week, or Sunday, as a holy day. The law setting apart Sunday as a day of rest or holy day was made by the Catholic Church long after the Bible was written, hence said law cannot be found in the Bible." A. N. Dugger, Editor, *Church of God Advocate.*

Catholic

Question: "Which is the Sabbath Day?"

Answer: "Saturday is the Sabbath Day."

Question: "Why do we observe Sunday instead of Saturday?"

Answer: "We observe Sunday instead of Saturday because the Catholic Church, in the Council of Laodicea (336 A. D.) transferred the solemnity from Saturday to Sunday."

Convert's Catechism of Catholic Doctrine

The story continues

The issues were now clear to me. The Bible still commands us to observe only the seventh day of the week as holy. But by reason of church tradition, the vast majority of Christian denominations were choosing to worship on Sunday instead of Saturday. In spite of the irrefutable facts, even within their own ranks, many had chosen to violate the Scriptures.

As for myself, I had made the decision to rely on the Bible alone as my source for truth and guide for safety. I had read where Jesus had clearly stated that "For the sake of your tradition, you have made void the word of God" (Matthew 15:6, RSV). So with such evidence from all quarters of Christianity, and, more importantly, from the Bible itself, my wife and I decided to begin keeping Saturday, the seventh day Sabbath, as our day of rest and religious worship.

However, upon making that decision we were totally unprepared for the response we were to receive from friends and family who didn't understand our decision or why we had made it. These well-meaning people, who were so dear to us, tried to prove that what we had done in rejecting Sunday and keeping Saturday was wrong.

We could sense they were frightened that we were going off the deep end. We overheard one family member saying to another, "People's lives fall apart when they begin studying the Bible on their own."

But, whereas they perceived that we were treading into the darkness of religious extremism, we knew that we were but coming out of the dark caverns of worldly tradition. Of course, when truth has been long set aside and erroneous traditions have prevailed as society's standard, any deviation from custom back to the original truth is going to appear radical. But the Bible was our guide and had become to us exactly what it said it would—"a lamp unto our feet and a light unto our path."

Though it pained us to realize that we and our loved ones were now on different roads regarding this subject, each had to make their own decision. As for me and my wife, we had firmly decided to follow God's Word and obey His law, be the cost what it may. We believed that when Jesus said "If you love me, keep my commandments" (John 14:15, KJV), He meant exactly what He said and was referring to all ten commandments, including the fourth one. To us the old proverb had taken on new meaning—"Buy the truth, and do not sell it." And what is the truth? "Your law . . . all your commandments are truth" (Psalm 119:142, 151). Thus the fourth commandment regarding Sabbath worship was as a seed of truth that had taken root in our hearts and lives. Yet because the world didn't know, it couldn't understand.

CHAPTER NINE

No Life on
Planet Earth

It was one of those hectic days at the office, when it seemed as though the more you did, the more there was to do. Demands were on every hand, especially from the accountants, who were trying to close out the year-end business. Phone lines were continuously occupied, and yet, in the midst of it all, an unrelated phone call got through to me.

As I answered, I recognized a past acquaintance who sounded deeply discouraged. He related that his relationship with his live-in girlfriend had turned sour. Seven months earlier I had counseled him, trying to help him get his life straightened out. At that time he had just moved to a new area and was lonely for a lifelong companion. He had often made this need a matter of prayer.

I suggested that if he wanted a good wife, one who would fill his life with joy and happiness instead of pain and disappointment, he needed to be strategic in where he looked. "You'll never find the girl God has in mind for you at the bars and nightclubs," I told him. "Try looking at churches. And when you find one you think would be compatible, get to know her family. Watch how she treats those she already claims to love. Before rushing to know her physically, get to know her mentally and spiritually. See what kind of principles she lives by. If you do this," I assured him, "you'll know when you have found the right girl to marry."

"Good idea," he replied, "thanks for the advice; I'll remember it."

Several months passed before I heard from him again. Then he called one day all excited about a girl he had just met. "I know God has brought us together," he said. "She's a Christian, has a good job, and just a real sweet and good person." Then he added, "We've moved in together, and we know God has worked a miracle in bringing us together." The better part of wisdom told me not to say anything, for I knew that the experience this young man had entered into would prove to be a much better counselor than I. "Glad to hear from you, Tom," I said. "I'll be here when you need me."

And it didn't take long for this teacher called "experience" to give the lesson. Only a few short months went by until I took his call that hectic day in the office. The relationship had not turned out to be the "miracle" he had thought it was. Gently I told him, "Tom, the bottom line is that you can never expect God's blessing to be upon a relationship if that relationship is not firmly built upon the principles of His established law. When God says 'no fornicating or adultery,' that's what He means."

"You're right," Tom replied in a hurried tone of voice. "Well, I've got to get going. Take care of yourself, Keavin."

"Take care of . . ." I tried to say as he hung up the phone and hurried back to the laboratory of bitter experiences.

How many people there are who have to learn everything in the school of hard knocks, all because they won't heed the instructions given by the One who "in the beginning" created the institution of marriage.

But God's law is not just a guideline for successful human relationships. It is also to be used as a foundation for our relationship with God. The last six commandments instruct us how to successfully relate to humanity, the first four tell us how to build a genuine relationship with God. Yet humanity's unfaithfulness in following the last six, as is evidenced in this world of failed human relationships, is simply indicative of what's taking place in the relationships that many professed Christians have with God.

Spiritual adultery is widespread among the ranks of Christendom. Every week multitudes go to His houses of worship and profess Him Lord of their lives. They claim to be His people—Christians. Yet, like Tom, they refuse to incorporate the principles of commitment, as outlined in the Ten Commandments, into their lives.

But God is not the one who is unfaithful. The Old Testament prophet Isaiah prophesied that toward the end of earth's history there would be a people who would want to be called Christians while not wanting to make a total commitment to all that God requires of Christians.

Today, radio and TV preachers tell the people it is wrong to disobey God's Ten Commandment law, yet by their own example lead people to a violation of them. They preach boldly against disregarding nine of the commandments while they do their best to detour around the fourth one that says "Remember the Sabbath day to keep it holy." Instead of going against the strong current of church tradition and proclaiming the seventh day as the Sabbath of the Lord, they exalt the pagan Sunday in its place. Nowhere in the scriptures can such men prove that God has sanctified Sunday. Instead, the Scriptures refer to Sunday (the first day of the week) as one of the six working days (see Exod. 20:9, 10; Ezek. 46:1).

Thus Jesus has something to say to those who knowingly and willingly violate His holy Sabbath in order to keep a day man has pronounced sacred. Many pronounce Him Lord but go against their convictions of Sabbath duty in order not to appear different or ridiculous in the minds of today's counterfeit Christian world. To such He says (as He said about the Pharisees of old), "This people draweth nigh unto me with their mouth, and honoureth me with their lips; but their heart is far from me. But in vain do they worship me, teaching for doctrines the commandments of men" (Matt. 15:8, 9, KJV). The apostle James taught us that if we will knowingly break one of those commandments, then we have broken our relationship with God and are considered by heaven as transgressors of them all. Will He not say to such when it is forever too late to save them, "Why call ye me Lord, Lord, and do not the things which I say?" (Luke 6:46, KJV).

War against the saints

But the book of Revelation says that during this time of religious hypocrisy there will be a people (saints) who, while trusting in the "faith of Jesus" to save them, will also "keep the commandments of God" (Revelation 14:12, KJV). Not just one or two, or nine of the commandments, but all of them, including the fourth one regarding Sabbath observance. Revelation 12:17 tells us the dragon, which represents Satan, "was wroth with the woman [a symbol of God's true church], and went to make war with the remnant of her seed, which keep the commandments of God, and have the testimony of Jesus Christ" (KJV). Unlike many who profess and preach Jesus but who don't fully yield obedience to all His commandments, these people will.

They will not only preach the gospel by professing to love and serve Jesus but they give "witness" of that love by keeping all His commandments. Their witness will be so powerful that the world's system of counterfeit Christians will be seen in its truest contrast. They will not be able to refute the sound biblical arguments. Many will be won to the "saints'" side. This will infuriate those who for so long perverted God's Word, and they will pursue the same course of action the Jews did toward Christ. Using their powerful resources of church and state, these religious leaders will pass laws against the "saints" and make it enforceable by death. But the saints "loved not their lives unto the death" (Revelation 12:11, KJV). They patiently wait for God to save them from their oppressors. They remain unshakable in their obedience to God's laws. And the Sabbath commandment will remain dear to their hearts, for it is over this that they have been so persecuted. But, to them, it is the very commandment by which they know they have a true relationship with God, for they have read where He said, "Keep my Sabbath sacred and let it mark the tie between us—to teach you that I am the Eternal your God" (Ezekiel 20:20, Moffat).

The Lord will counteract the oppressive plans of the wicked by sending upon them the seven last plagues (see Revelation, chapter 16). With this event probationary time will have come to an end. The world will then enter "a time of trouble, such as never was since there was a nation, . . . and at that time your people [God's faithful] shall be delivered, every one who is found written in the book [of life]" (Daniel 12:1, NKJV). Yes, at that time Jesus will be preparing to make His return to this earth and rescue those who, even in the face of death, took their stand for Him.

When Christ finally does appear, the righteous will look up and exclaim, "Behold, this is our God; we have waited for Him, and He will save us" (Isaiah 25:9, NKJV), while those who rejected Him will be terrified by His approach. In shadows of their own guilt they will run to the dens of the earth and cry out to the rocks saying, "fall on us and hide us from . . . the wrath of the Lamb" (Revelation 6:16, NKJV). Then as Christ draws near to the earth they will be slain by His brightness (see 2 Thessalonians 2:8; Revelation 19:21).

At that time Christ will gather unto Himself His elect from all corners of the earth. "For the Lord Himself will descend from heaven with a cry of command, with the archangel's call, and with the sound of the trumpet of God. And the dead in Christ will rise first; then we who are alive, who are left, shall be caught up together with them [those risen from the dead] in the clouds to meet the Lord in the air; and so we shall always be with the Lord (1 Thessalonians 4:16, 17, RSV).

And where will these saints then go? To find the answer to that question we must investigate what the Bible teaches concerning a 1,000-year period of time commonly referred to as the millennium.

The millennial reign

The second advent of Christ will usher in the period of earth's history known as the millennium. At that time those people redeemed from the earth will go to heaven and there "they lived and reigned with Christ a thousand years" (Revelation 20:4, KJV). We know heaven is where they will go because when Christ was ending His earthly ministry and preparing to return to heaven He told his disciples, "In my Father's house are many mansions; if it were not so, I would have told you. I go to prepare a place for you. And if I go to prepare a place for you, I will come again and receive you to Myself; that where I am, there you may be also" (John 14:2, 3, NKJV). The Bible refers to this physical redemption of the saints as the first resurrection. "Blessed and holy is he who has part in the first resurrection. . . . they . . . shall reign with Him a thousand years" (Revelation 20:6, NKJV).

But prior to Christ's return, the earth will be battered by the seven last plagues. Needless to say, with such devastation the entire earth will be left in total ruin. Then upon Jesus' return, any wicked left alive will be slain by His brightness. The defilement of their own lives renders them incapable of living in God's presence. By choice they are forever now attached to their sins, and to sin, God's presence is a consuming fire (Hebrews 12:29). But the living righteous will be protected and taken to heaven for 1,000 years.

The Old Testament prophet Jeremiah saw this time in vision and carefully described it, "I looked on the earth, and lo, it was waste and void; and to the heavens, and they had no light. I looked on the mountains, and lo, they were quaking, and all the hills moved to and fro. I looked, an lo, *there was no man*, and all the birds of the air had fled. I looked, an lo, the fruitful land was a desert, and all its cities were laid in ruins before the Lord, before His fierce anger" (Jeremiah 4:23-26, RSV, emphasis supplied).

During this 1,000-year period, God will confine Satan to this desolated, uninhabited earth. There will be "no man" whom he can practice his deceptive arts upon by tempting him to sin. He will be left alone to an existence of inactivity for 1,000 years, and now he must contemplate the role he has played in the great universal drama of sin. While left in this condition he has nothing to do but look forward to "a fearful prospect of judgment, and a fury of fire which will consume the adversaries" (Hebrews 10:27, RSV).

This is the scenario John relates to us: "Then I saw an angel coming down from heaven, holding in his hand the key of the bottomless pit and a great chain. And he seized the dragon, that ancient serpent, who is the devil and Satan, and bound him for a thousand years, and threw him into the pit, and shut it and sealed it over him, that he should deceive the nations no more, till the thousand years were ended" (Revelation 20:1-3, RSV). The pit spoken of here is the desolated earth. The chains by which Satan is bound represent the circumstances that bind him and prevent him from practicing his business of tempting people to sin, for there will not be any left alive on earth for him to tempt.

The saints' work during the millennium

Immediately after John saw Satan being bound to the earth, he said, "Then I saw thrones, and seated upon them were those to whom judgment was committed." He went on to tell us who these were that the work of judgment was committed to, "the souls of those who had been beheaded [or killed] for their testimony to Jesus and for the word of God, and who had not worshiped the beast or its image and had not received its mark on their foreheads or their hands. They came to life again, and reigned with Christ a thousand years" (Revelation 20:4, RSV). The ones doing the judging are none other than those saints who were redeemed from the earth. At this time they will have their part in the judgment of Satan, his angels, and the lost inhabitants of the world. It was this time the apostle Paul had in mind when he wrote: "Do you not know that the saints will judge the world. . . . Do you not know that we are to judge angels?" (1 Corinthians 6:2, 3, RSV; see also 2 Peter 2:4 and Jude 6).

We should understand that this millennial judgment by the saints is not for the purpose of deciding who will be saved or lost. That decision will have already been irrevocably made by each person who has ever lived. Instead, the purpose of this special phase of judgment is primarily to aid the saints in answering any questions they might have pertaining to why the wicked are lost. It is to clear up any remaining doubts concerning God's fairness.

They will know that God did all He could to save their loved ones. Though it will be hard for them to accept, they will know that their earthly companions are lost because they themselves had refused eternal life.

End of the 1,000 years

The end of the millennium will usher in another sequence of events. The time will have arrived when God will finally put an end to the sin problem. It will be the last confrontation between the powers of good and that element called evil.

It begins with the descent of Christ out of heaven, along with His saints and the city of New Jerusalem, back down to the plague-ravaged earth. John the revelator said he "saw the holy city, new Jerusalem, coming down out of heaven from God" (Revelation 21:2, RSV). Please take note that this will be the third coming of Christ to the earth.

The stage will then be set for the last battle between Christ and Satan to take place. Remember, for 1,000 years Satan has been chained in his prison house of circumstances by having no one to deceive. John had told us that after being bound at Christ's second coming, "he should deceive the nations no more *till the thousand years were finished*. But after these things [the 1,000 years] he must be released for a little while" (Revelation 20:3, NKJV, emphasis supplied). Since Satan had been bound in that he had no living humans to deceive, he will be "released for a little while" due to the fact that Christ at the end of the millennium will resurrect all the wicked dead back to life. Speaking of this second resurrection of humanity John said, "The rest of the dead did not live again until the thousand years were finished" (Revelation 20:5, NKJV). Thus "when the thousand years have expired, Satan will be released from his prison" (Revelation 20:7, NKJV) by the resurrection of the wicked. The great deceiver will be temporarily back in business. And take notice that he wastes no time. He "will come out to deceive the nations which are at the four corners of the earth . . . to gather them for battle; their number is like the sand of the sea" (Revelation 20:8, RSV). What an incredible sight! All the wicked people who have ever lived upon this earth assembled into one vast army with Satan as their commanding general.

As Satan gathers his forces, he inspires them with the hope that they can, by force, capture the great Holy City and overthrow its righteous inhabitants. "And they marched up over the broad earth and surrounded the camp of the saints and the beloved city" (Revelation 20:9, RSV). The very fact that the wicked, upon receiving life again, will once more turn against God and His people gives final confirmation to all that the decision God has made concerning their fate was correct. These creatures, whom He originally made in His image and for whom He died, have become hopelessly maddened by the terminal disease called sin. And now out of love and mercy toward His pitiful creation, God must once and for all end their miserable existence.

This is the time of the Great White Throne Judgment. As God's enemies surround the city with plans to attack it, every human who has ever lived will be gathered together in that one place. Paul referred to this time when He wrote, "We shall all stand before the judgment seat of Christ" (Romans 14:10, NKJV). All those who are saved will be safe and secure within the city while those who are lost will be raging with envy outside its gates. Jesus prophesied concerning this experience of the lost, "There you will weep and gnash your teeth, when you see Abraham and Isaac and Jacob and all the prophets in the kingdom of God and you yourselves thrust out" (Luke 13:28, RSV).

Up until now the wicked have been judged by others. But in this last judgment scene they will pass judgment on themselves. They will confirm by confessions from their own mouths that God's ways have been just. Paul said, "At the name of Jesus every knee should bow, in heaven and on earth and under the earth, and every tongue confess that Jesus Christ is Lord" (Philippians 2:10, 11, RSV). The entire human race, both the saved and the lost, and even Satan himself, will on that day bow on their knees and confess Christ to be the only true God. All the questions concerning this great spiritual controversy, all those lies about God that began when Lucifer rebelled in heaven, will be answered and seen in their truest light. Satan will be recognized as a force whose greatest desire was to kill God, along with everything that stands for what's good and right. In contrast, God will be understood for what He really is—a fair and loving Creator who was willing to give up His own life to save His lost creatures. Now God, with the full request and consent of all creation, can unquestionably put sin and those who are eternally and incurably contaminated by it to an end by means of an eternal death.

The lake of fire

Immediately after the wicked confess that God is just and receive the sentence of their eternal fate, they will make one last, desperate attempt to storm the city. But as they make their advance toward its massive walls, "fire came down from heaven and consumed them . . . this is the second death, the lake of fire; and if any one's name was not found written in the book of life, he was thrown into the lake of fire" (Revelation 20:9, 14, 15, RSV). As fire comes down from God out of heaven, the earth will be literally broken up. The petroleum weaponry that has been concealed in its depths will burst forth. The fire ignites these powerful fuels, and devouring flames leap from every yawning chasm. Earth's elements, the rocks, water, even the atmosphere, are all on fire. The day has come that shall burn as an oven. These elements will melt with intense heat; the earth also, and all the works established by men are burned up (see Malachi 4:1, 2; 2 Peter 3:10). The earth's surface seems one red hot, molten mass—a vast, seething lake of fire. It is the time of judgment and perdition of ungodly humans.

But while the earth is wrapped in this fire of destruction, the righteous abide safely in the Holy City.

Upon those who had part in the first resurrection, the second death now has no power. While God is to the wicked a consuming fire, He is to His people both a sun and shield.

"I saw a new heaven and a new earth, for the first heaven and first earth had passed away" (Revelation 21:1, NKJV). The same fire that consumes the wicked also purifies the earth. Every trace of the curse will be forever swept away.

Thus Satan and sinners, the root and branches of sin, will come to their final end. They die the second death from which they can never be brought back to life. They will never exist again. There will be no eternal tormenting of their pitiful souls. God, out of necessity in protecting the universe from the contagious and destructive presence of sin, will have brought them to their final state of nonexistence, and universal justice will have been maintained. As for sin itself, God has declared it will never raise its ugly head again. All the inhabitants of the universe will understand the true nature of sin and will never want anything more to do with it. God's eternal kingdom will forever be secure from sin and its destructive tyranny.

The new earth

"I then saw a new heaven and a new earth; for the first heaven and the first earth had passed away" (Revelation 21:1, NKJV). After this earth has been cleansed by fire, God will, in the sight of all the redeemed host, re-create the earth back to it's original beauty, as it was before sin defiled it. This cleansed, re-created earth will then become the eternal home of the redeemed. The promise of Jesus will be fulfilled. "Blessed are the meek, for they shall inherit the earth"

(Matthew 5:5, NKJV). After He re-creates the earth, Jesus will swing open the gates of the great city and the saved from among men will venture out for the purpose of homesteading their own eternal piece of real estate. The righteous, who have been won back from the land of the enemy by His blood "shall inherit the land and dwell therein forever" (Psalm 37:29, KJV). As we walk across the earth's surface, the wicked will be ashes (dust) under the soles of our feet (see Malachi 4:3). However, for the saints, the past is forgotten. "God Himself will be with them; he will wipe away every tear from their eyes, and death shall be no more, neither shall there be mourning nor crying nor pain any more, for the former things have passed away" (Revelation 21:3, 4, RSV). These blessed pilgrims won't remember anything about their sinful past or of their loved ones whom sin destroyed. They will have received perfectly new, glorified bodies at the Second Coming (see Philippians 3:21). Only one visible evidence of the horrors of sin will remain, that being the marks and scars made upon the body of the lovely Jesus at Calvary. Only by this will the redeemed be reminded of the destructive nature of sin. But while He bears the marks of pain, the saints' reward will be peace, happiness, and contentment throughout the eternal ages.

As for our new homes, Paul tells us that "Eye has not seen, nor ear heard, nor have entered into the heart of man, the things which God has prepared for those who love Him. But God has revealed them to us through his Spirit" (1 Corinthians 2:9, 10, NKJV). But even with the revelation of God's Spirit, no human language can adequately paint the eternal paradise. The only people who will ever realize what it is really like will be those who actually make it there.

However, we can let our imaginations try to picture what it will be like through glimpses provided in the Bible. According to Revelation 21 and 22, we will all have a private mansion in the city called New Jerusalem. That city itself has four walls, each being 375 miles long, 20 stories high, and all made of solid jasper. In each wall there are three massive gates, each one being carved out of a single pearl. There will be no need for sunlight there because the place is radiated by a glorious light proceeding from God Himself. The streets are made of gold. A gigantic river of life, not with muddy waters like rivers here on this old earth but with waters that are as clear as crystal, will flow within its holy banks through the city and empty into an enormous sea of glass. Bridging the river is a tree whose trunk extends to both sides of the river and joins at the top. It is the famous tree of life we have heard so much about while on earth. The tree yields twelve different varieties of fruit, one for each month of the year. The nutrients contained in this fruit are so powerful that they provide its partakers with eternal vitality. Oh, just imagine, dear friends, what it is going to be like to live there.

We will also have a home in the country where we will plant vineyards, orchards, and gardens and eat the fruit of our pleasant labors. As we look across the meadows, whose grass glistens like the purest silver and whose flowers never fade, we will watch our children playing among the peaceful wildlife of the place. "The wolf also shall dwell with the lamb, the leopard shall lie down with the young goat; the calf and the young lion and the fatling together; and a little child shall lead them" (Isaiah 11:6, NKJV). Everyone and everything shall be at peace, "for the earth shall be full of the knowledge of the Lord" (Isaiah 11:9, NKJV).

One of my favorite things to do here on this earth is travel to new places. In the earth made new, whenever we desire, we can travel freely to other worlds that are the homes for various orders of intelligent creatures, all created by our great Jesus. They are all willful servants to Him. Think of it: an eternity to explore the unimaginable beauties of God's vast creation!

Whatever it is, dear friend, that we think is so great and grand down here on this sin-defiled earth will not even begin to compare with what God has planned for us in heaven and the earth made new. With such a prospect laid before us, should we not now carefully consider the injunction given by Peter as he contemplated the destruction of sin and the glories of the eternal kingdom. "What kind of people ought you to be? You ought to live holy and godly lives as you look forward to the day of God and speed its coming. That day will bring about the destruction of the heavens by fire, and the elements will melt in the heat. But in keeping with his promise we are looking forward to a new heaven and a new earth, the home of righteousness. So then, dear friends, since you are looking forward to this, make every effort to be found spotless, blameless and at peace with him" (2 Peter 3:11-14, NIV).

CONCLUSION

One of the most famous stories in the Bible tells of a prominent man in his community who comes under conviction that God is going to destroy the entire world with a massive, universal flood. This fear moves him to liquidate all his financial investments and quit his job in order to have time to build a boat designed to ride out the storm. He begins to warn his friends and family so they, too, might prepare. However, most only laugh and make fun of him. They think he is a deluded religious fanatic, someone who has irresponsibly thrown his life and career away. Still others privately wonder if there might be some validity to what this man is doing, but they shrink from joining him for fear that what others are saying about him would be said of them.

One hundred twenty years later, this man, along with seven people who have believed what he said, boards the finished vessel. Then rain falls from the sky, and the great reservoirs of water in the earth break forth with unrelenting force, deluging the entire earth's surface with floodwaters. Everyone except those aboard the boat lose their lives.

As it was in the days of Noah

First, Jesus said, "Just as the world was in Noah's day, that's how it will be immediately before I come back. All that people thought about was eating, drinking, getting married and living it up. They did this right up to the very day that Noah and his family went into the ark" (Matthew 24:37, 38). In other words, people were totally given over to serving their own self-interests. As a result, men's knowledge of committing evil reached such a height of frightening, out-of-control proportions that God was forced to check the overwhelming tide of wickedness. Finally, He decided to send a flood to slow the acceleration of sin in the earth.

God never destroys arbitrarily. It is not His desire that any should perish, but that all would turn from their wrongdoing and learn to do right. Yet for the best interest of the universe there comes a time when God has to say, enough is enough! There is a point when humanity takes their sins to the place where there is no hope of returning to what is just and good. There is a time when the shedding of innocent blood in places like Rwanda, the starvation of the masses because of greed in places like Africa, the abduction of innocent children in places like America, and man's inhumanity under the cloak of religion the world over, must cease. There does come a time when God has to affirm people's final rejection of good and their love for evil by touching the earth with His merciful hands of judgment. Yet before He ever does this, God always sends a warning so those who truly want to do what is right may have opportunity to escape the ruin. He sends them a messenger who warns about the coming judgment and gives instruction on how to avert it. In the antediluvian world, that messenger was Noah.

As for Noah himself, he was not superhuman. He simply believed that what God said was going to happen would happen. And he not only believed but he acted upon his belief. God had given Noah explicit directions on how to build the boat, and Noah obeyed and did whatever God told him to do. If there was anything extraordinary about this man, it was that he obeyed God's instruction in the face of ridicule and humiliation from the world around him. He put everything he had—money, time, labor, and reputation—into building that ark, thus giving indisputable evidence he had faith in God's leading. People could say a lot about Noah, but the one thing they couldn't say was that he didn't practice what he preached. Think about it: What good would Noah's preaching of a coming flood have done if the people didn't see him preparing for it—if he had just joined them in their status quo lifestyles and attitudes? Instead, every blow of his hammer upon that ship preached a sermon of the urgent need to get ready.

For 120 years Noah pleaded with the people to join him in making preparation for the great event. But the Bible says that the people were too occupied with fulfilling their lifelong dreams and ambitious plans. Although Noah prayed and wept over them, they still didn't have the time or interest to listen. So on that fateful day when Noah entered the ark, only seven people who believed what he had preached boarded with him. Only seven, out of a whole world's population! Yet Noah, still hoping someone else would believe, preached as long as there was any time left. The New Testament records that God "spared not the old world, but saved Noah, the eighth person, a preacher of righteousness, bringing in the flood upon the world of the ungodly" (2 Peter 2:5, KJV). For the people and their ambitious dreams, time had run out. The hour of their probation had expired.

So shall it be . . .

So, therefore, we realize the seriousness of what we are talking about when we read that Jesus, describing the way life was in the days of Noah, said "that's how it will be when the Son of Man comes back" (Luke 17:30). Regardless of what we want to think, the desires that dominate the human heart have not changed. We like to tell ourselves we are smarter and more sophisticated than were those people back then; but when it really comes down to it, we have the same basic needs and concerns— what we eat, what we wear, where we live, whom we marry, how we appear to others, and what we can do for fun. These are the things that motivate the vast ranks of humanity. Most spend their whole life's energy in pursuit of them.

In describing the way life was in the days of Noah, just before the world was destroyed by the Flood, Jesus said, "Just as the world was in Noah's day, that's how it will be immediately before I come back. All that people thought about was eating, drinking, getting married and living it up. They did this right up to the very day that Noah and his family went into the ark" (Matthew 24:37, 38).

One may understandably argue that there was nothing wrong with what the people were doing. After all, what evil is there in eating or in getting married? While in and of themselves these things are legitimate and good, the problem arises when we become so obsessed and absorbed with them that we fail to recognize the signs of intended warning God has given. Most devote their whole lives to getting more and more of the perishable things of this world. Greed, passion, jealousy, envy, and selfishness become the controlling impulses of life. And men and women literally become slaves to their own wants and lusts. Thus they build their kingdoms in this world and are found unprepared when God comes knocking on the door in judgment. Little do they realize that all the while a loving God is waiting to give them something better!

It certainly doesn't take much discernment to see that in the last fifty years our society has been drastically transformed by the very conditions Christ predicted would dominate at the end of time. Excesses in eating and drinking today are evidenced by the rampant increase of lifestyle-related diseases such as heart disease, diabetes, and cancer. Even in the midst of the AIDS epidemic, the promulgation of homosexual rights and lifestyles is continuing to the point that Ruth Graham, wife of evangelist Billy Graham, stated, "If God doesn't do something soon He will have need to apologize to Sodom and Gomorrah." Many young people marry and try to live better than their parents did. They build homes and lifestyles they will spend most of their lives paying off or will later divide in a divorce court, their marriages destroyed because of stress incurred by their unwise decisions. Parents seem more preoccupied with making money, the next pleasure party, or who wins the ball game, than they are with the eternal destiny of their children. Thus the doctors, lawyers, entertainers, and conscience-easing ministers get rich through the neglect of individual responsibilities and duties.

This is not what God intended for human living. By example, Jesus outlined a better plan for living. That plan calls for a total forsaking of so-called worldly customs and traditions, and a building of new values upon different principles of life.

Although this plan may appear foolish in the eyes of worldly people, those who finally make the unpopular decision to give their whole lives in following God's design for living will reap the reward of peace, contentment, true happiness, and eternal joy. The first principle to be learned is that this present world is not the believer's home.

When Adam sinned, this world came under the dominion of Satan. Coming into this world we were all automatically born under his jurisdiction. This world was our home. Its ways of thinking and principles of survival were all we knew. Then we heard about God's plan for a better life at the end of this one, and through acceptance of Christ's sacrifice at Calvary, we met the conditions of that plan. But many fail to comprehend that upon becoming Christians we are no longer to consider ourselves citizens of this world but ambassadors to it. We have received a new birth by a new Father! Heaven is now our home because it is His. Our only purpose for existing here is not to build up earthly estates and bank accounts but to be busy trying to get people to go home with us.

It is this truth that an early twentieth-century American missionary came to realize one day. He had been serving God faithfully for many years in Africa and was finally on his way home to America. He soon learned that President Theodore Roosevelt was aboard his ship returning from a hunting safari. As they pulled into New York harbor, masses of people lined the docks with signs saying, "Welcome Home Teddy." The bands were playing while the people cheered. It was a glorious event.

As the travel-worn missionary made his way down

the plank, not one person was there to greet him. Feeling friendless and forsaken, he made his way down a lonely, narrow street. As the excitement faded from his ears, he cried out with tears in his voice, "Why, Lord? I've spent all these years serving You, and no one cares enough to even come welcome me home." But the immediate response from his heavenly Father quickly brought him back to the reality of who he was. God simply replied, "That's because you're not home yet!"

One of the first lessons a new Christian needs to learn, and never forget, is that this world is not his home. True Christians consider themselves "strangers and exiles on the earth. . . . they desire a better country; that is, a heavenly one" (Hebrews 11:13, 16, RSV).

That's the way it was with Jesus. He said, " 'My kingdom is not of this world' " (John 18:36, NIV). To the professing religionists of His day, who were all caught up with their earthly desires and passions, He said, " 'You are of this world; I am not of this world' " (John 8:23, RSV). Because they refused to give up the hopes they had established in this world, they ended up crucifying Him.

It was the understanding of who Christ was and what He came for that opened the eyes and hearts of His early followers. Jesus had been the ruler seated upon the throne of the heavenly universe. He had power over all creation. It was envy toward Him that opened the floodgates for sin in the hearts of angels and then men. But because He loved this world so much, He left all His loved ones in heaven to become a man. He followed a lonely, sorrowful path in the land of His enemies to show them the way back to heaven.

Throughout His life here, He was constantly criticized and misunderstood by His earthly friends and family for being different. He knew that His mission was not to please them, not to join them in their blindness of mind—eclipsed by worldly traditions—but to show them a better way that would ultimately lead back to eternity with Him. He came to rescue them from the pit of a lost world that is spinning toward ruin. To them He said, as He still says to us today, " 'If anyone desires to come after Me, let him deny himself, and take up his cross, and follow Me' " (Matthew 16:24, NKJV). We will realize just what that cross is when we truly follow the Saviour to the point we are misunderstood as He was. Then we will not lead others to invest their aspirations in this earth's future but will by precept and example point them to Christ as "the way, the truth, and the life" (John 14:6, NKJV). As a result, the world won't know us, because it didn't know Him.

Here in the end time the gospel message of Christ is to cut people away from the way the world thinks and what the world does. Jesus cautioned us, "Don't follow the crowd. The pathway to destruction is wide and well traveled. There are comparatively few who are really interested in finding the way to heaven" (Matthew 7:13, 14). This, my dear friends, is the way it always has been and always will be in a sinful world with its magnetic attractions. If we ever find the true God and His road to heaven, we are going to discover that the traveling companions are few.

Satan knows all this, so he tries to deceive those interested in Christianity with a false gospel. He would like to have us believe that anyone who makes any profession of faith without a drastic change in life and thought is on the road to the heavenly paradise. He sends people who appear to believe and teach heavenly truths, but their teachings do not lead away from the world's practices. These teachers are actually anti-Christian. Speaking of these false teachers Jesus said, " 'Some spiritual leaders seem to be very interested in the things I'm telling you, but you can't always be sure which way they are leading you' " (Matthew 7:15). The apostle John warned of them this way, "These false teachers are influenced by the way worldly people think, and that's why they teach the way they do. Worldly people listen to them because they, too, are influenced by the way the world thinks" (1 John 4:5). As a result, much of the so-called Christian world is nothing more than worldly-minded people who profess to be following the meek and lowly Galilean.

All such deception is about to end. The battle between the powers of good and evil in this world is about to consummate. A worldwide crisis will soon come and test the true character of every man and woman to make manifest which side he or she is on. The gospel message of salvation through Christ's merits alone, which lead to obedience to all God's commandments, will do its work in separating the true followers of Christ from those who merely profess their loyalty to Him. This message is now being heralded in nearly every nation of the world. Concerning its proclamation Jesus said, " 'This gospel of the kingdom will be preached in all the world as a witness to all the nations, and then the end will come' " (Matthew 24:14, NKJV). Notice that He said it only had to be preached in all the world, not accepted by all the world.

The decision on our part to accept or reject this gospel will help in answering a question Jesus posed one day. He asked, " 'When the Son of Man [Jesus] comes, will He really find faith on the earth?' " (Luke

18:8, NKJV). In other words, when Jesus returns, will there be anybody on earth who will be like Noah and go against the world's popular tide to be ready for the coming calamity? Jesus asked this in a questioning manner because He understood that to possess genuine faith, one is required to love God and His truth more than anything else in this world—be it money, position, fame, appetite, or if necessary even one's own parents, spouse, or children. He knew the power these things had in controlling the human race. But though these things will continue to motivate and intimidate the world's population, they will have no power upon those who find true faith.

Miraculously, some will escape the shackles of bondage which we call "the norms of society." They will have pondered carefully the thoughtful question, " 'What profit is there in gaining the whole world and all the good things of this life if it causes you to lose your own soul and forfeit eternal life?' " (Mark 8:36). They will have made some difficult, unpopular decisions in order to forsake what this world is offering. They will have devoted their entire lives to preparing themselves and others for the Lord's coming.

I ask you, dear reader, will you stand firm for what you know to be right, or will you bow to the world's pressure? I know it is a difficult decision, but I encourage you to take your stand against the popular trends of this world, as did Noah. If you will make the choice to follow God, even in the face of the world's opposition, then He will be with you just as He was with them. He will send you His Holy Spirit and then, dear friend, you will know by experience how to "become more Christlike and to live above the evil desires that are corrupting this world with lust" (2 Peter 1:4).

I'd rather have Jesus than silver or gold,
I'd rather be His than have riches untold;
I'd rather have Jesus than houses or lands,
I'd rather be led by His nail-pierced hand.

I'd rather have Jesus than men's applause,
I'd rather be faithful to His dear cause;
I'd rather have Jesus than world-wide fame,
I'd rather be true to His holy name.

Than to be the king of a vast domain
Or be held in sin's dread sway;
I'd rather have Jesus than anything
This world affords today.

-Rhea F. Miller

If you enjoyed this book . . .

and would like to receive additional materials or information, simply indicate your choices, print your name and address, then tear out this page and mail it to:

Truth That Matters
P.O. Box 5353
Nampa, ID 83653-5353

___ I would like to purchase a copy of *The Desire of Ages*, the classic book on the life of Christ. (Enclose check or money order for $3.50, payable to Pacific Press.

___ I would like a **FREE** set of Bible study guides.

___ I would like information concerning a free seminar on the book of Revelation in my area.

___ I would like a list of other books published by Pacific Press.

___ I would like **FREE** information on other literature related to the topics contained in this book. (These offers good in the United States and Canada only.)